Make it Paleo

over 200 grain-free recipes for any occasion

Bill Staley and Hayley Mason

authors of *The Food Lovers Primal Palate*

[www.primal-palate.com]

VICTORY BELT PUBLISHING INC.

Las Vegas

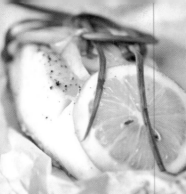

First Published in 2011 by Victory Belt Publishing.

ISBN 13: 978-1-936608-86-7

This book is for educational purposes. The publisher and authors of this instructional book are not responsible in any manner whatsoever for any adverse effects arising directly or indirectly as a result of the information provided in this book.

Victory Belt ® is a registered trademark of Victory Belt Publishing Inc.

Printed in USA
RRD 1211

Foreword

by Mark Sisson

When Bill and Hayley first sent over a draft of their recipe book and asked me to write the foreword, I was incredibly honored, but hesitant. You see, I have a couple recipe books on the market myself, and from the looks of it, they were going to give me a run for my money. The recipes were simple and looked delicious. The pictures were clear and professional. The instructions were concise and well written. They even provided strong justification for why you should eat primal. This book had it all.

Then I tried a couple of the recipes myself, and got even more concerned. The food just disappeared from my family's plates. I couldn't recall any of my dishes being such hits.

I'm kidding, of course. Well, not about the praise, but rather the hesitancy of my support. Heck, I've been linking to their recipes on my blog as long as they've been around. Random readers kept sending me links to this "great new primal recipe blog." Once I checked it out, they were in the regular rotation. And, after all, this world needs all the primal/paleo recipe books it can get, especially one as well done as *Make it Paleo*. For all the simplicity of this lifestyle—and really, what's simpler than following a biologically appropriate way of eating and moving?—people trip up over the smallest things. People need to know what to make for breakfast and how to choose cuts of beef or how to handle an omelet. Well, this book does all that.

What I like about this book is that it's a celebration of food, first and foremost. The primal/paleo angle is important, but it's not the main selling point. The quality of instruction, description, photography, and—most importantly—gustatory delight is what sets this book apart. You don't even have to be on a primal diet to get something out of it. It's just good, real food. Real food that just so happens to be incredibly healthy without obstructing your digestion, perforating your intestinal lining, fattening your liver, spiking your insulin, and leaving you hungry two hours later, but in the end it's just food that anyone can cook and enjoy.

Bill and Hayley remind me why I keep plugging away with the blog. Because as many people as we hear about who get healthy and take themselves off the meds doing this primal thing, it's great knowing that people are also using it to reinvent other aspects of their lives. These two are a young couple taking charge of their own finances and health by doing something they love. They're turning passion into a viable product that people want—and, more importantly, need. I don't know about you, but that sounds like the American dream to me, as silly and outdated as the concept might be, and it gives me hope.

Okay, enough from me. I'll be planning my next recipe book and hoping that it measures up to this one. As for you guys, start reading and get cooking!

Mark Sisson
author of *The Primal Blueprint*
blogger at MarksDailyApple.com

Contents

Breakfast

Appetizers

Entrées

176

242

228

198

SEAFOOD

246

Salads

Soups

Sauces & Dressings

316

318

328

324

312

336

348

336

334

352

Side Dishes

Treats & Cheats

366

364

378

374

386

412

414

390

394

432

Introduction

One of the biggest concerns many people have when transitioning to a grain-free lifestyle is the daunting thought of a complete dietary change. Perhaps, more accurately, it is the fear that many favorite foods will no longer be permitted. We've carefully crafted every recipe in this book with that concern in mind. We want to inspire you to cook great meals, without the worry that you'll feel something is missing from your plate.

Let us show you how to *Make it Paleo*.

Introduction

A Note from the Doctor

I believe it is poetically just that I introduce this book. I am Hayley's grandfather. I feel at least partially responsible for introducing her to the importance of good food and good diet.

I became a nutritionally oriented MD in the early 1970s, long before such behavior was acceptable in most medical circles. I then introduced my eldest child Julie (Hayley's mother) who was then dragged, kicking and screaming, into what became Hayley's modern world of nutritional consciousness. Of course this foreshadowed Hayley's birth. This foreshadowing ultimately played a key role in the evolution of Hayley and Bill's marvelous recipe book. The rest of Julie's family, consisting of Julie's siblings, Uncle Josh, Aunt Jenny, and Aunt Justi, and their mother, Kyp, also played a part. It would seem simple nowadays, but believe me, these were turbulent seas that we sailed, and they still are in some ways.

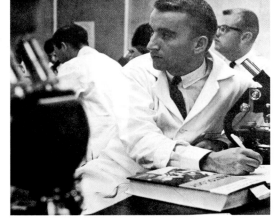

Hayley heard the frequent family discussions on the power of nutrition. I'm recounting how Hayley's mother and her siblings were sent to birthday parties with their own cake in a brown bag. Of course, they trashed the nutritious cake as soon as they could, and ate the same sugar loaded stuff with the other kids. Peer pressure you know. Nevertheless, they became aware of the power of nutrition and the paradigm shift that is now giving us somewhat of a choice. We do not have to settle for poor-quality food. The quality of our food supply is polarizing. At the good pole, organic and high-quality foods are becoming more available even as the junk food and coffee bars at the other pole become more ubiquitous. But at least we have a choice.

When our family was young, we got pretty intense with food selection. We pitched all the gelatins and boxed cake mix and white bread. We found an organic farm in Arkansas. Every month, Shiloh Farms delivered to us, from a refrigerated eighteen-wheeler, a month supply of frozen organic food. We had two 25-cubic-foot freezers to accommodate this bonanza. I think that this contributed to our overall health. It certainly showed that we were different from our neighbors when it came to food.

Even though I focused much of my medical skills on choosing a great diet, it was still difficult for me and most health professionals. And, of course, then as now, broad disagreement among experts confounded the issue of what is the best diet. From Dr. Carlton Fredericks, I learned about the Seale Harris Diet for hypoglycemia. I then used a wide range of diets, including the Atkins Diet, Pritikin Diet, Ornish Diet, Stillman Diet, South Beach Diet, HCG Diet, Mucusless Diet, etc. etc. I have used almost all of the diets, even when they were not fashionable. One could easily argue that the paleo diet makes the most sense. It addresses many health issues in a positive way. Hypoglycemia (low blood sugar) for example, is a form of subtle malnutrition that we manage best with a low sugar, low refined carbs, low alcohol, low caffeine, etc. The paleo diet immediately satisfies those needs and mollifies the fatigue, brain fog, and other upsetting symptoms. This strategy in turn decreases the inflammatory response from an irritated immune system.

I have given nutritional counseling to over 20,000 patients in the last four decades, dealing with almost any health problem imaginable. Many of them would not have needed me if they had eaten a paleo diet.

Hayley and Bill's paleo recipe book can introduce you into the old caveman's world of eating intuitively and nourishingly. If the sword has two edges, it only has one direction. It only cuts in your favor. It gives you delicious food and a healthy body to relish it.

I now introduce a book that needs no introduction. Welcome to Hayley and Bill's paleo cookbook, *Make it Paleo*.

- Murray Susser MD
"Grandpa Buz"

Our Story

How We Became *The Food Lovers*

"Everything happens for a reason." "Thoughts become things." "A failure only leads you in the directions of success." "This is the law of attraction." Many of you have heard some of these sayings before. Where we are today is a direct result of all of those philosophies. We met on the set of a music video, and many of you have heard this story before. Bill, the drummer. Hayley, the makeup artist. Neither of us had a clue that a year from the day we met our lives would revolve around cooking, eating, and sharing our food with others, or that we would eat, sleep, and breathe our blog and be up until all hours of the night working on the website together, revising recipes, writing blog posts, editing photos, and researching new recipe ideas together. Neither of us knew that we would be publishing a cookbook together before our second year anniversary. We were two strangers, doing what we loved the most, playing music and painting faces. To really get a feel for how *The Food Lovers* came to be, we are going to share the story of how it all started from each of our points of view.

Hayley's Story

For years I felt as if I were battling with my body. Constantly on a mission to "lose weight," I always felt as though it was harder for me than everyone around me. I tried numerous fad diets and cleanses in high school, through which I saw short-lived success, only to be followed by binge eating of junk food due to the overly restrictive food choices. I do, however, believe that any struggle is a journey and a lesson to guide each of us to our ultimate goal. Looking back on it all, my "obsession" with my physical appearance along with

the knowledge I had of healthy eating from growing up in a wellness-oriented family is what led me to the paleo/primal way of eating. The whole paleo movement is such a mindful way to eat and live, and through it all I have really been able to appreciate myself, and my body. For the first time in my life, I feel balanced, happy, and relieved of stress and anxiety around food. For me, and others who come from a background of dieting, retraining the body and mind to live a healthy lifestyle is a continuous process. There is freedom for me now in knowing that I have found a way to eat and live for my entire life, and not just for a few weeks without knowing what should come next. I know that not only am I feeding my body the foods that it was designed to eat, but I am consuming the highest-quality foods in those categories. Moving my mind-set from "what should it look like from the outside" to "this is what my body needs and deserves" creates a whole new context that is empowering and self-motivating.

I was first introduced to the paleo diet, not too long before I met Bill. I had heard of the diet from a good friend of mine, the owner of CrossFit Confluence here in Pittsburgh, Patrick Benton. I was vegetarian at the time, and although I considered myself to be a healthy vegetarian since I did not consume gluten and limited sugar intake, I was certainly not looking so good or feeling so good. When Patrick first mentioned the diet, I was a bit confused and thought it was just a high-protein diet filled with meat. As he explained a bit more to me, it began to make sense; however, I was not entirely convinced that it was "for me." I was still hanging on to the idea that the vegetarian lifestyle was what I wanted. I finally decided to add chicken back into my diet and remove all grains, and I immediately felt and saw a huge difference. I had also learned that my cousin Steven had been eating a paleo diet for about ten years, so I was really anxious to talk with him about it. I had recently lost around twenty-five pounds on another diet that was very restrictive. I was happy

that my body was looking the way I wanted it too, but I was hungry and miserable and knew I couldn't live my life that way. I started to make some more changes with my eating in the way of adding some more fat into my diet, and immediately felt better. One day, through a quick Google search for "almond flour pancakes," I was lead to Marks Daily Apple. I found myself searching through Mark Sisson's website day and night for hours on end, absorbing as much information as I could. The

more research I did, the more I realized that the diet I was eating to maintain my weight loss was the actually the paleo diet, or Primal Blueprint. When talking with my cousin, I became very inspired as he explained more about the philosophy behind this way of eating. After losing weight from adding back in animal protein and eliminating grains, and then learning the philosophy behind the diet, I was hooked. I easily maintained my weight loss, and felt better than I ever had before. I knew this was the way I wanted to live my life.

The day I met Bill, my entire world shifted. I did not realize at the time that this shift was occurring, but it was. I was the girl who had always wanted the fairy tale romance but had convinced myself that it was only make-believe and could never be a reality. I was almost convinced that there wasn't anyone out there for me; however, in the back of my mind there was hope. I could visualize that special someone. I knew what I deserved, and as many times as I told myself I didn't deserve it, in the back of my mind I knew the truth. Thoughts become things. Every path, good or bad, leads you in the direction you need to go. I am a true believer in that. Sometimes the current reality seems hopeless, but it always takes you where you need to go, or teaches you what you need to know to take yourself in the right direction.

The week I met Bill, I made a decision to myself to let go of everything that was holding me back. I didn't want to settle anymore. I wanted what I knew I deserved. I didn't know how or when it would show up, but I knew it was coming. Within days of my new mind-set, he walked into my life. I was doing the makeup for the lead singer of his band for their music video, and he was there playing the drums. We spent fifteen hours together on the set, and although we didn't talk much, the times that we were talking felt as if we had known each other our entire lives. In the short period of time spent together, we knew that we both felt strongly about health and fitness, we were both artists, and we were both passionate about what we do. I of course thought that this relationship would turn out like all the rest, into a friendship, but he had something different in mind.

When we started dating I introduced Bill to the paleo diet. I was eating this way most of the time, but still splurging on conventional treats from time to time. Bill was convinced that due to his high metabolism and desire to keep weight and muscle on he couldn't eat a full paleo

diet, even though it made sense to him with barely any explanation. We cooked meals together, but I would make a serving of rice for him, or send him off to work with a bag of organic oat cereal. Even with the modified paleo diet that he was eating, he was still starting to see great results, and he was starting to feel a lot better. It wasn't until we spent a weekend at the beach, and he had three days of strict paleo eating with me, that he realized this was it. He was hooked. To this day, I am still impressed by his ability to accept an alternative way of eating/lifestyle, first just because he loved me

and would support me in anything that I do, but also because it made sense to him from the beginning. He didn't need convincing, he didn't need research. He just knew that this was right. On that trip, we started photographing our meals that we were making together. We were at the beach, enjoying the sunshine and eating fresh local produce and seafood. We would look forward to each morning when we would get up and drive to the local farmers market to get just enough produce for that one day. One evening over dinner, Bill, deep in thought, looked at me and said, "Let's write a cookbook!" My first reaction was, okay! But after taking it in for a moment, I responded with, "Let's try a blog first." Bill, always in support of me, agreed without hesitation (I still don't think it has sunk in how absolutely blessed I am to have found him), and that was the birth of our website *The Food Lovers' Primal Palate*.

Our journey is far from over. We have both grown so much as a couple and as individuals through the growth of our website. From the day we started our website, we made a commitment to ourselves and each other that we were going to take on the primal way of eating 100 percent. This was now how we wanted to live our lives together. Since that day, we haven't looked back once. We are constantly learning, and eager to learn and gain more knowledge of the lifestyle we are living. We do hope to inspire others to make healthy changes as we have. I, especially, hope to encourage other women, men, young girls, and children to step back from the harsh body images of the world we live in today and to appreciate and love yourself. When you come from a place of love and respect of self, everything else falls into place. I have been there; I know it's challenging, but just knowing that I am doing the best that I can to take care of my body, not just make it look better, is so much more rewarding. The way I consider all of the lessons is just a bonus.

Bill's Story

I grew up in a family that always strove to eat healthy foods (conventionally speaking). At a young age, my mother had me in the kitchen helping her make dinner—I suppose I was her little sous chef. Part of the reason I loved being in the kitchen was having access to pots and pans, which I could bang on with chopsticks. Twenty years later, I'm still banging on things—but now I'm getting paid to do so, and on stage, no less. The other part of the reason I loved being in the kitchen was to be able to sample whatever my mom was making at the time. Even though I hung around for cookie dough and impromptu jam sessions on a set of pots, I somehow managed to pick up some cooking skills in my childhood years.

A lot of the recipes I introduce in this book talk about meals my family used to enjoy when I was growing up. Food was always a pillar of family life. Each night, the four of us would gather around the kitchen table and enjoy dinner together. It sounds corny or perhaps unbelievable by today's standards, but this nightly ritual was a huge part of my life growing up. I loved the food my mother used to make, and a lot of the food I still love to eat is a reinvention of dishes she fed us when I was a kid. I would be remiss if I didn't attribute

my love of food to my mother, not only because she helped me appreciate good food, but also because of the love that can surround it, especially how it can bring a family together.

It wasn't until college and the years after that I learned how to truly cook. My skills were first put to the test

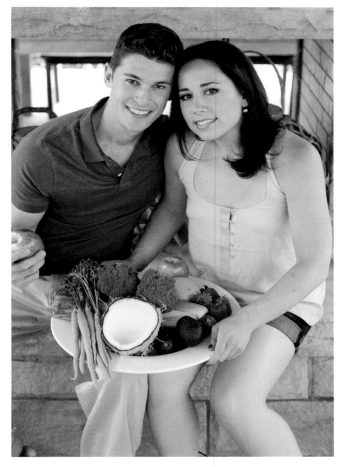

in my early twenties as a young bachelor living and entertaining in Washington, D.C. I remember how my first paycheck was spent: a picnic table, a keg of beer, and a big grill. I suppose that, in a nutshell, perfectly describes my priorities in those first few months out of school. Later that summer, though, I really got into weight lifting and fitness. A roommate of mine had been lifting for years and showed me the ropes. I was instantly hooked. The rush I felt every time I got a good pump was addictive. I became a gym regular and lifted three to four times a week (sometimes more). I didn't necessarily ditch my partying ways, but it was the beginning of a conscious shift toward a healthier lifestyle—a shift that would ultimately take a few years to fully root.

In late 2008, I moved back home to Pittsburgh from Washington, D.C., to take a new job in landscape architecture, the field I studied at Penn State. At the same time, I got in touch with an old musician friend, Anthony Rankin, to see if he knew of any local bands in need of a drummer. Having played drums for fifteen years, I figured it would be a fun and creative outlet for me after long days at the office. Anthony said his drummer was moving away and that he needed me in his band. To this day I'm still "Ace," the rhythm man in Anthony's band.

By now, you know that Hayley and I met on the set of a music video shoot. She was hired to do Anthony Rankin's makeup, and I was (of course) playing the drums in the video. I'll never forget the moment I really noticed how special she was: she said she was incredibly sore from doing deadlifts the previous day. You could say it was love at first sight; I never knew any girls who could deadlift. Not surprisingly, we instantly connected that day and talked much about eating and living healthy in the following weeks. When we started dating, I began to shift my eating habits—slowly eliminating all the processed foods, sugars, grains, and dairy in my diet.

During a long beach weekend in July, 2010 I decided to go full paleo, as Hayley was already eating that way. The whole concept of evolutionary eating made perfect sense to me, and besides that, I never really cared for pasta and bread all that much anyway.

For the first six weeks, I regularly lost a pound or two. I wasn't necessarily looking to lose weight, but it was hard to argue with the results in the mirror: I was clearly getting some nice definition! The primal diet I had assumed was burning away fat, helping to reveal my hard-won muscles from years of working out.

Hayley made my transition to primal eating so easy, always having great ideas for meals that never felt like compromises. We would often talk excitedly about things we could make together. As you might imagine, these conversations are still a high point of our relationship. They can strike us at any time—while we're at the gym, out on a walk, or even just driving around—but I can always tell when she has a great idea brewing.

Eating a paleo diet has allowed me to burn off fat and add muscle at the same time, and I feel better than I ever have. At the gym, my time is focused on developing "useful strength." I occasionally do CrossFit workouts, and enjoy trying other types of exercise as well (à la Primal Blueprint fitness). I guess you could say that it's more for feeling good than anything else.

I'm so grateful to have Hayley as a partner in this whole adventure. We are a great team, and definitely have the yin and yang aspect going for us. Having the support of a loved one in eating an ancestral diet is very helpful. We are constantly encouraging and supporting one another. It is truly a blessing to have found one another. As the saying goes—you will find the person you are meant to be with when you stop looking for her or him, and simply start doing the things you love.

What Is the Paleo Diet?

The paleo diet is based on the idea of eating the foods our bodies were designed for through thousands of years of evolution. These foods were available to early people through hunting and gathering [meat and fish, nuts and seeds, fruits and vegetables]. During modern times, advances in technology have made other forms of food available for consumption [grains, dairy, and processed foods], which are not as easy for our bodies to digest. The foods recommended in the paleo diet generally provide our bodies with more efficient, long-lasting energy that also aid in burning fat.

Primal | Paleo

"Primal" generally refers to Mark Sisson's Primal Blueprint way of eating, which is very similar to paleo, but allows some leeway with certain types of dairy and has fewer restrictions on saturated fat intake. Throughout this book, we use "paleo" and "primal" as interchangeable terms. Generally speaking, the paleo diet is a high-protein, moderate-fat diet, and the Primal Blueprint is considered to be a high-fat, moderate-protein diet. Many people who follow this way of eating consider the terms to be one and the same. However you personally decide to "title" the ancestral diet that you abide by, both stem from the core principle of eating the foods our bodies were designed to eat: plants and animals.

Enjoy	Avoid
Meats	Grains
Vegetables	Legumes
Fruits	Dairy
Nuts	Processed Foods
Seeds	Alcohol
Healthy Fats	Starches

Beyond the guidelines

Eating paleo is not a cut and dry affair. Sure, the guidelines provide an easy to remember set of rules that you can recall in a snap. However, in our minds the paleo diet is more about intuitive eating. In other words, you should be actively thinking about what you are eating. To start, read any and all food labels. Are there ingredients that are not natural? If so, then it likely isn't your best choice.

Beyond the lists of do's and don'ts, it is occasionally acceptable to eat full fat raw dairy, starchy vegetables, and natural sugars. However, if you are looking to feel the maximum health benefits, eating a strict paleo diet with only whole foods and minimal treats will be your best avenue to success.

The Paleo Kitchen

Now that you have a grasp of the paleo diet, your next question is probably, "Okay, well what do I eat?" Here is where we come in. In this section we are going to map out how to shop for groceries and stock your pantry for successful grain-free cooking. The first step in this matter is to discard (or donate to a food pantry) all the food that you are no longer going to consume.

This may seem confronting, but how does that saying go? Ah yes, out of sight, out of mind, right? If it is not in your cupboards, you will not think of it. You want to set yourself up for success if you are truly trying to shift your lifestyle to a healthier one. Get rid of it all. Your skin, sleep, energy, and overall total well-being (oh and don't forget your abs!) will thank you. Even toss that last bit of oatmeal or whole-grain bread; that's right, get rid of it. The next step is to fill your kitchen with all that you need to successfully create grain-free dishes. This can be as simple or as detailed as you would like. The majority of what you will be making will consist of fresh foods, and you will need a few key staple items for the cooking.

For this section, we are going to list the products that you will want to have on hand at all times. These staple items are the ones in our kitchen, and they are what you will be using to create every recipe in this book.

Meat and Fish

When purchasing meat and fish, you really want to make sure that you are investing in a quality product. As a part of the grain-free lifestyle, you also should make sure that the animal protein you are eating comes from animals that were fed a diet that they were meant to consume. Consuming animals that were raised in appropriate conditions will only contribute to your health, and support the health of our planet. As a rule of thumb, look to buy organic grass-fed meats, wild-caught fish, and pasture-raised poultry. If available, it is also best to purchase your meat directly from a farmer. This way you will be supporting local farming, and you will be sure of the quality of the product you are buying. When purchasing fish, take into account endangered fish, and avoid purchasing fish that are threatened. Part of making good food choices is knowing what you are buying.

Meat

Always choose grass-fed/pasture-raised organic meat when possible. If grain-fed is your only option, look for a leaner cut of meat, so as not to consume toxic fat stores of grain-fed animals.

- Beef
- Lamb
- Bison
- Pork
- Venison

Poultry

When choosing poultry, pasture raised is best. This will mean that you are consuming poultry that was allowed to roam freely and feed off of bugs and other insects. Organic, free-range chickens are the next best thing to pasture-raised if you do not have access to local farm-raised chickens. A free-range organic chicken is a happy, healthy chicken that will contribute to your health and happiness as well.

- Chicken
- Turkey
- Duck
- Pheasant
- Goose

Eggs

If you cannot find a local source of pasture eggs, your best option is to enjoy omega-3-enriched eggs. Pasture eggs come from chickens that feed freely on bugs. Omega-3-enriched eggs come from chickens that are fed a vegetarian diet, but supplemented with flax to increase their omega-3 content.

Seafood

When choosing seafood, it's always best to choose wild-caught fish. Similar to meats, wild-caught fish will be your best option for obtaining a good amount of omega-3 fatty acids naturally from food. It is also best to choose nonendangered fish that are caught using sustainable and ethical fishing practices.

Our top ten seafood options to enjoy:

- Alaskan Salmon
- Yellowfin Tuna
- Mahi Mahi
- Shrimp
- Scallops
- Clams
- Oysters
- Mussels
- Crab
- Lobster

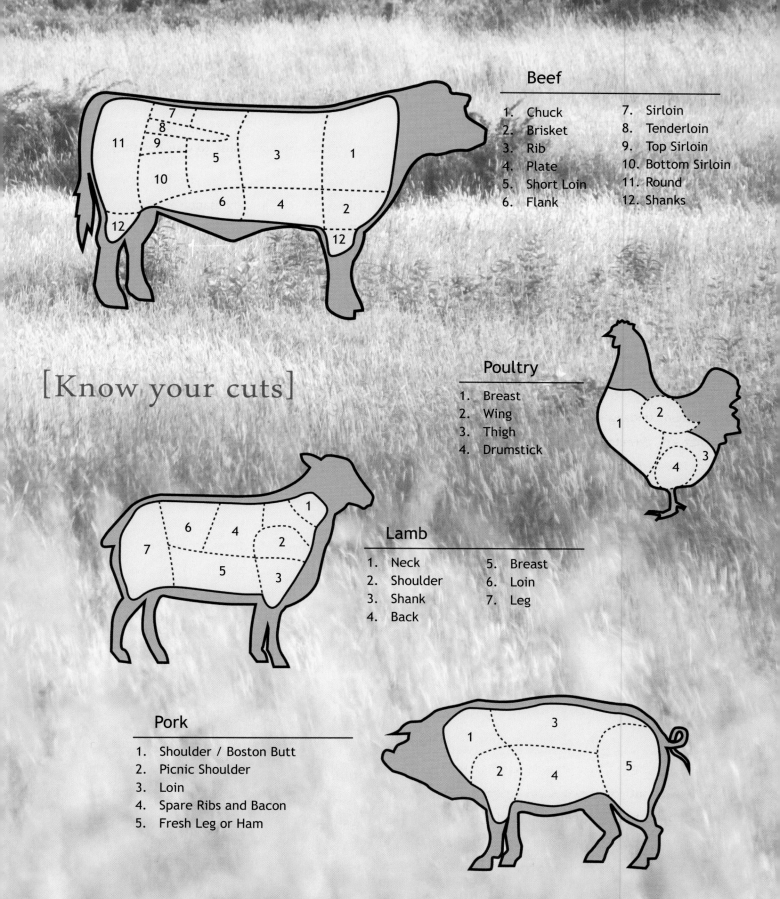

Beef

1. Chuck
2. Brisket
3. Rib
4. Plate
5. Short Loin
6. Flank
7. Sirloin
8. Tenderloin
9. Top Sirloin
10. Bottom Sirloin
11. Round
12. Shanks

[Know your cuts]

Poultry

1. Breast
2. Wing
3. Thigh
4. Drumstick

Lamb

1. Neck
2. Shoulder
3. Shank
4. Back
5. Breast
6. Loin
7. Leg

Pork

1. Shoulder / Boston Butt
2. Picnic Shoulder
3. Loin
4. Spare Ribs and Bacon
5. Fresh Leg or Ham

Fruits and Vegetables

You will find a large array of fruits and vegetables in this book. We are big fans of growing our own produce, or getting it at a local farmers market when possible. In many parts of the Northern Hemisphere, that means late April through October. Another way of receiving fresh produce is by participating in a CSA (community supported agriculture) program.

Through a CSA, a farmer sends his or her best crops to a specified drop point near you. This is a great way to support local family farms. In general, it is important to be aware of how your fruits and vegetables are grown. If buying produce directly from a farmer or farmers market is not an option, then look for organic and pesticide-free fruits and vegetables in your local grocery store.

If you have a green thumb and a sunny spot, you can try your hand at growing your own herbs and vegetables. Even if you do not have a yard, it is relatively simple to propagate some basic herbs in a small planter on a sunny window sill. If you have a yard, even better! We like to grow lettuce, beets, broccoli, peppers, and a whole slew of herbs (lemon thyme, thyme, rosemary, basil, oregano and chives to name a few!) There is no better salad than one with fresh veggies from your garden. To complete the circle of sustainable gardening, we take non-meat table scraps and compost them in an effort to continually improve the soil.

But what if you do not have time to tend to a garden, and there are no farmers markets nearby? That's okay, because there are often plenty of options in your local grocery store. When shopping for fruits and vegetables, it is often better to buy organic items, because they will have the least amount of chemicals and pesticides involved in their production.

Certain crops tend to absorb pesticides more than others. Consider buying these fruits and vegetables pesticide free (organic) whenever possible:

- Strawberries
- Spinach
- Bell peppers
- Nectarines
- Lettuce
- Pears
- Apples
- Celery
- Peaches
- Cherries
- Grapes

As a final note, we recommend buying your produce in season. It'll be cheaper, easier to find, and will taste incredible when freshly picked. Here is a brief list of seasonal vegetables. Although your selection will vary by region, these general guidelines will help you create great dishes year round.

Seasonal Produce

Spring

apricots	mint
artichokes	mushrooms
asparagus	parsley
grapefruit	radishes
green onions	rhubarb
leeks	spinach
lemons	spring onions
lettuce	strawberries
maple syrup	wild greens

Winter

beets	mandarins
Belgian endive	onion
cabbage	parsnips
celery	pears
citrus	Pomelos
clementines	rutabagas
escarole	sweet potatoes
horseradish	turnips
kiwi	

Summer

apples	garlic
avocado	green beans
basil	mangoes
bell pepper	melons
berries	nectarines
carrots	okra
cherries	peaches
cilantro	peppers
cucumbers	summer squash
eggplant	tomatoes
figs	zucchini

Autumn

arugula	kale
broccoli	lemongrass
Brussels sprouts	limes
cauliflower	pomegranates
collards	pumpkin
chilies	shallots
cranberries	Swiss chard
curly endive	winter squash
fennel	
grapes	

Oils and Fats

Healthy fat is an essential component of the paleo diet. Many vital bodily functions depend on the presence of healthy fats in your diet. Here we outline many of the healthy sources of these fats and how they relate to primal cooking. All of these oils and fats can be found in local health food stores, online, or in better grocery stores.

Unrefined Virgin Coconut Oil

This is our primary cooking oil. We use this oil for most of our cooking done on the stove top and for any grain-free baking. Coconut oil is solid at room temperature. We find it is best to use this oil to sauté vegetables, fry eggs, and use in baked goods. It adds wonderful flavor to dishes, but does not have an overpowering coconut flavor, which makes it ideal for most cooking.

Coconut Butter

Similar in consistency to a nut butter, coconut butter is simply coconut oil with the meat of the coconut mixed in. Coconut butter is great to add to sauces, stir-fries, smoothies, or to top apples, bananas, celery, carrots, or berries.

Red Palm Oil

Red palm oil is virgin and unrefined. This is your best choice when purchasing palm oil. Palm oil has a distinct flavor with warm undertones and rich red color. Pairing this oil with dishes can be tricky, because it will change the color of the food slightly, and it is best suited for international cuisine. The flavor is wonderful and can surely enhance any dish. For first-time use, try frying up some eggs with red palm oil; you won't be disappointed!

Palm Shortening

This vegetable shortening, derived from palm oil, is a staple item for all of our grain-free baking recipes. It essentially has no flavor or smell, and is wonderful in grain-free pie crusts or whipped frostings. We often use palm shortening in place of coconut oil in our cookie recipes, pie crusts, and muffin recipes.

Ghee

Ghee is clarified butter, meaning the milk solids (or proteins) have been removed, resulting in pure fat. You can use ghee in place of butter or oil in a recipe. Ghee is available at most health food stores but can simply be made at home by

simmering grass-fed butter until the solids have settled at the bottom and a froth has appeared on the top. Carefully remove the froth, and spoon out the ghee without disturbing the solids at the bottom.

Grass-Fed Butter (Pasture Butter)

Another fantastic fat to use in cooking. It is labeled "grass-fed" because it is produced from the milk of grass-fed cows. Butter is fantastic over steamed vegetables, used in sautéing, roasting vegetables, as well as for basting poultry when baking or roasting.

Lard

Lard is derived from the fat of pigs. You can easily render your own lard by saving bacon grease in a glass jar, and keeping it stored in the fridge for any time you would like some delicious bacon-flavored eggs or vegetables.

Tallow

Tallow is rendered beef fat. This saturated fat is incredibly heat-stable, which makes it ideal for any high-heat cooking. With a fairly mild flavor, tallow is fantastic for cooking any vegetables, as well as browning meats.

Olive Oil

Our primary oil to make salad dressings and marinades, olive oil is a liquid at room temperature, but will solidify when chilled. Olive oil is not as heat stable as saturated tropical fats or animal fats, so we do our best to limit olive oil to cold uses.

Avocado Oil

Used only as cold oil for salad dressings, its creamy flavor is wonderful over any salad. Just a drizzle along with a splash of fresh lemon juice or balsamic vinegar adds amazing flavor.

Macadamia Nut Oil

This oil is our favorite choice to create homemade mayonnaise. Macadamia nut oil has a very mild flavor, with just the slightest hint of sweetness and warmth. You can also use this oil for a simple salad dressing as well.

Sesame Oil

Derived from sesame seeds, this oil has a relatively high smoke point and is a good choice for moderate heat applications. Its distinct sesame flavor lends itself well to Asian dishes, and can be used as cold oil for dressings.

Nuts and Seeds

Nuts and seeds are a fantastic garnish to a dish, as well as a great snack when you are in a pinch. Offering a good amount of protein and fat, a small handful of nuts or seeds can keep hunger at bay for quite some time. To obtain the most nutritional benefit from nuts and seeds, it is best to consume them raw, or even better to soak them overnight and then dehydrate them (pg 80). In this book you will see the use of nuts and seeds mainly as a garnish in recipes, but more prominently in our grain-free baking. Nut flours and nut butters make fantastic grain-free substitutes for conventional wheat flour when baking.

Add nuts and seeds to salads to enhance flavor and texture, sprinkle over soups, create your own raw trail mix, or just grab a small handful when you need a quick bite. Here are some of our favorite nuts and seeds for snacking as well as to garnish dishes:

- Almonds
- Walnuts
- Pecans
- Macadamia nuts
- Sunflower seeds
- Flax seeds
- Pine nuts

You can essentially make a nut butter out of any nut you desire. These are great to spread over fruit or vegetables, as well as added to sauces or dips. Nut butters can create a tasty grain-free treat as well. Our "go-to" nut butters can be made at home, or purchased at your local grocery store or health food store:

- Almond butter (pg 316)
- Sunbutter (pg 316)

Nut flours are one of the staple ingredients that we use in our grain-free baking recipes. We found the use of nut flours to be best suited for cookies, pie crusts, pizza crusts, and crackers.

Blanched Almond Flour

This almond flour is very fine due to the skin of the almond being removed. This nut flour will result in a very smooth-textured baked good, very similar to conventional flour.

Almond Meal

This is a coarser almond flour due to the skin of the almond being ground into the flour as well. You can make almond meal at home by grinding raw almonds in a food processor. Almond meal works fine for all grain-free baking, but the end result will not be as flawless as when using blanched almond flour.

Flax Seed Meal

Flax seed meal is simply ground flax seeds. These can be used to sprinkle over salads, or add to grain-free baked goods to create a more "earthy" flavor. We typically use flax seed meal when we want to make something a bit more savory such as our "n'oatmeal raisin cookies" (pg 362), pizza crust (pg 164), as well as grain-free crackers (pg 94).

Pecan Meal

Pecan meal is simply ground raw pecans. This nut flour is one that we have made at home using our food processor. Pecan meal is our first choice when making a grain-free pumpkin or apple pie.

Herbs, Spices, and Seasonings

Spices and fresh herbs bring life to your dishes. We want our dishes to be enhanced by herbs and spices, but not overpowered by them. A little goes a long way, and fresh is always best. To keep waste to a minimum, you can freeze any leftover fresh herbs for future use. When in a pinch, you can refer to our "go-to" seasonings here:

Poultry	Pork	Lamb	Seafood	Beef
herbs de Provence	garlic	rosemary	lemon	garlic
garlic	rosemary	thyme	lime	onion powder
onion powder	oregano	oregano	garlic	coffee
shallot	paprika	garlic	onion powder	cinnamon
parsley	smoked paprika	onion powder	parsley	cumin
lemon	fennel seed		Old Bay seasoning	smoked paprika
thyme	cumin			paprika
rosemary				chipotle
basil				
oregano				

Other Key Ingredients

When stocking a primal pantry there are other ingredients that are helpful to have on hand for most cooking endeavors. As your palate evolves through your own personal primal journey, you will find certain ingredients that you prefer to keep on hand, but for now we will supply you with some of our favorites for you to use as a base.

Coconut Aminos

Coconut aminos are a fantastic alternative to soy sauce. We will often use coconut aminos to season meat or fish, as well as to add to dressings and marinades. Coconut aminos come from the sap of the coconut tree, have a slightly sweeter flavor than soy sauce, and are also less salty. Coconut aminos are available at most health food stores, as well as online.

Fish Sauce

Fish sauce is another great way to add big flavor to dishes. Be cautious when purchasing fish sauce, because many contain sugar or other undesirable ingredients. Be sure to read labels. Your best bet is an extra-virgin fish sauce that only contains fish and salt.

Brown Mustard

Spicy mustard, or Dijon-style mustard is an ingredient that you will find in several of our recipes. This is one that we use for dressings, marinades, or steak rubs. When purchasing Dijon-style mustard, always read the ingredients. Many contain sugar or wine. When purchasing brown mustard, look for a brand that contains these ingredients: mustard seed, apple cider vinegar, spices, and salt.

Coconut Milk

Coconut milk is one ingredient that you will want to have on hand. You can use coconut milk as cream in coffee or tea; to add to sauces, curries, soups, and marinades; as well as in homemade smoothies. You will even find coconut milk as the base for all of our ice cream recipes in this book, as well as primal pudding. Coconut milk is available at most grocery stores, but can very easily be made at home (pg 84).

Almond Milk

Almond milk is another staple item that we like to have on hand when possible. Similar to coconut milk, we prefer to make our almond milk from scratch (pg 84), but you can also purchase almond milk at your local grocery or health food store. It is best to opt for unsweetened, plain almond milk, since this will result in no added sugars or undesirable ingredients. Almond milk is fantastic over grain-free granola (pg 80); can also be added to soups, smoothies, homemade ice creams, and used as a creamer for coffee or tea.

Unrefined Sea Salt

When eliminating processed foods from your

diet, you will also naturally be eliminating a lot of sodium from your diet. We use salt sparingly, and only during cooking. It is very rare for us to add salt to a dish after it has been cooked. When choosing to add salt to dishes, it is best to opt for an unrefined natural sea salt. This will offer fantastic flavor to your dishes, without any chemical processing.

Broths and Stocks

Broths and stocks are very simple to make on your own, as shown on pg 300. Making homemade bone broths are a great way to bring minerals and nutrients into your diet. Nothing quite says comfort like a hot cup of homemade stock. The use of store-bought stocks is found in this book as well. For those recipes we use Imagine Organics brand. This brand carries low-sodium stocks without sugar and has very few ingredients. Any recipe in this book that calls for stock can be replaced with a homemade bone broth.

Dehydrated Coconut
(flaked or shredded)

These are great to have on hand to add to trail mix or simply as a snack on their own. You will find shredded coconut in a few of our grain-free baked recipes, but dehydrated coconut is fantastic with savory dishes as well (see pg 64 for coconut-nested eggs).

Coconut Flour

When creating grain-free baked goods, coconut flour is our top choice for making cakes, muffins, and cupcakes. Coconut flour is a very dense flour, so you will use a very small amount of flour in recipes along with more eggs. This will result in a fluffy "cake" like dessert. You can also use coconut flour as a binder in crab cakes or meat balls, as well as a breading for shrimp or chicken. Coconut flour is also a great way to thicken sauces or gravies. A little goes a long way with this product.

Vinegars

Vinegars are often found in dressings and marinades. In this book you will see the use of Balsamic, White Balsamic, Raspberry Balsamic, as well as Apple Cider Vinegar. Most dressings that call for vinegar can easily be replaced with the fresh juice of a lemon or lime. Apple Cider Vinegar unfiltered and raw is your best choice for using vinegar, however the smell and flavor is very strong. We do not use vinegars often, but they are fine in moderation for flavor purposes.

Thickening Agents

We don't use thickening agents too often in recipes, but when we do we choose guar gum, gelatin, or coconut flour. You will see the use of gelatin in some of our pies and puddings. When choosing a gelatin, always opt for unflavored. Guar gum can be found at most health food stores and can be slightly tricky to use. When using guar gum, you want to start out with a very small amount and slowly blend it into the food. Using too much too fast will cause it to clump and prevent it from evenly distributing throughout. Coconut flour easily thickens sauces, but again less is more. A little goes a long way with coconut flour.

In The Kitchen

Tools that make primal cooking a bit more civilized

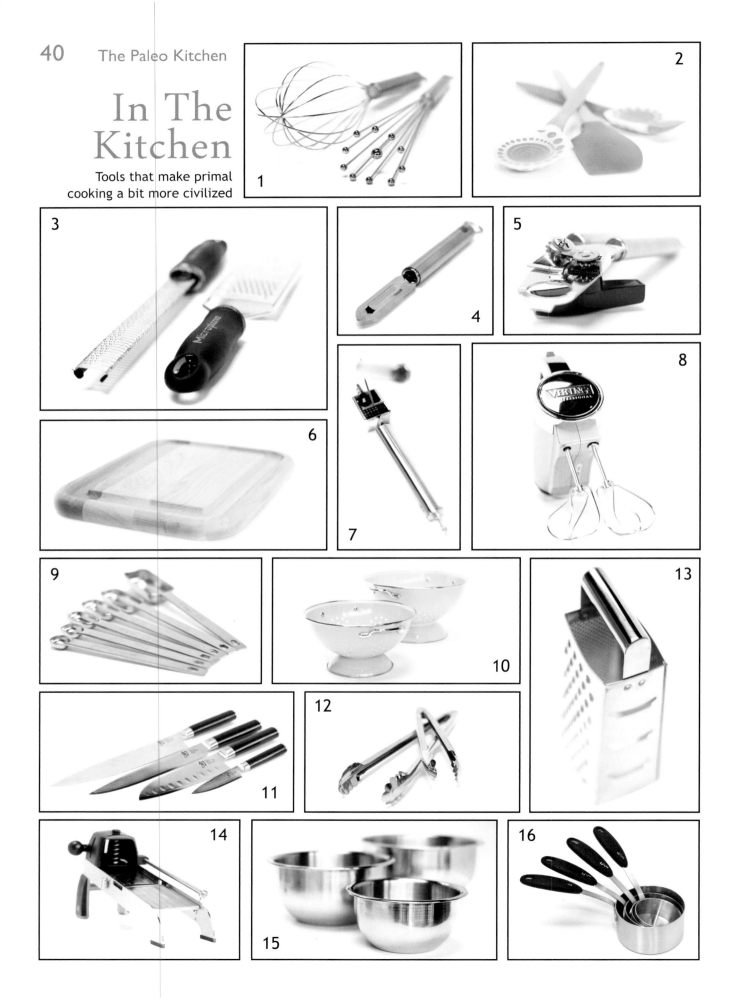

1

2

3

4

5

6

7

8

9

10

11

12

13

14

15

16

1. Whisk
2. Silicone scraper
3. Microplane
4. Vegetable peeler
5. Can opener
6. Cutting board
7. Garlic press
8. Hand mixer
9. Measuring spoons
10. Colander
11. Assorted knives
12. Tongs
13. Cheese grater
14. Mandoline
15. Mixing bowls
16. Measuring cups
17. Dutch oven
18. Assorted pots
19. Slow cooker
20. Meat thermometer
21. Blender
22. Loaf pans
23. Baking sheets
24. Grill wok/plate
25. Baking dish
26. Wok and skillet
27. Kitchen mixer
28. Nonstick pans
29. Food processor

Basic Cooking Tips

We have a few very simple rules for cooking. As you will see from our recipes, we use a lot of tried-and-true flavor pairings and utilize generally simple cooking methods. These tips are a few simple guidelines for cooking that we continue to use every day. Whether you are just learning your way around the kitchen or are a seasoned cook, these simple instructions are ones to keep in mind for any cooking endeavor.

Don't be afraid of your food

Get in there and get dirty. Mix with your hands; touch the raw meat or fish. It's okay, so long as you wash up afterward! Fearing the food is one sure way to limit your cooking abilities. For some it can be scary or "gross" to really get in there and cook with your hands, but it is really empowering once you start.

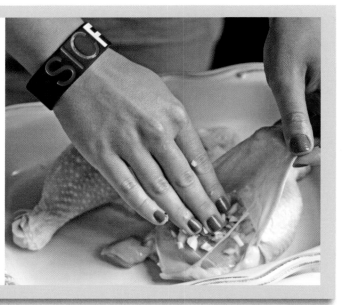

Practice makes perfect

Make the same recipe a few times over until you get the feel for it. Once you get the hang of things in the kitchen, you can experiment with more complex recipes, or even making a few recipes at a time. Pick one skill to work on and master it, whether it's sautéing, baking, or grilling.

Less is more

We are all about getting big flavor, but we typically use simple flavor pairings. You'll find that many of the best tasting recipes in this book use five ingredients or less. This approach allows the true flavors of the food to shine. The idea is to enhance the natural flavors, not cover them up.

Pay attention while cooking

Ovens, stoves, and grills all perform differently from one another. It is best to keep an eye on your food as it cooks to make adjustments to cooking time if necessary. Eventually you will just know that your oven runs cool, or your grill has hot spots. (Here, our friend Mike, "the Traveling CrossFitter," shows great grilling technique by carefully monitoring his asparagus.)

Have some fun

There are few things in life as simple and fulfilling as making some great food and then eating it. Cooking should be a low-stress activity. To keep your kitchen stress free, it often helps to read the recipe fully first (so there are no surprises), and to prepare a few things ahead of time.

Breakfast

Breakfast is our favorite meal of the day. One that we are fortunate enough to share together almost every morning. As our palates have evolved through our journey in the paleo lifestyle, we have seen the most significant change in our breakfasts. Here we invite you to "break fast" with us, as we take you through our journey.

Eggplant hole in the head

One of our favorite breakfasts growing up was the classic hole in the head with a slice of bread. For this recipe we used grilled eggplant in place of the bread. This has quickly become one of our favorite breakfasts.

Ingredients

- 1 large eggplant
- 1 tbsp extra-virgin olive oil
- 1 tsp pasture butter or coconut oil
- 4 eggs
- Salt and pepper to taste
- 1 green onion, sliced

Difficulty:

Prep Time: 10 minutes

Cook Time: 20 minutes

Serves: 2-4

Process

1. Preheat grill to high heat.
2. Rinse the eggplant, then cut into 1-inch-thick slices from end to end.
3. Brush eggplant slices with olive oil, sprinkle with salt.
4. Grill eggplant for approximately 3-4 minutes per side.
5. Cut a hole in the center of each piece of eggplant using a small circular cookie cutter.
6. Sauté eggplant in frying pan over medium heat with pasture butter (or coconut oil). Crack egg into center of eggplant slice.
7. Allow egg to cook for 3-4 minutes, then flip carefully.
8. Cook for an additional 2-3 minutes.
9. Add salt and pepper to taste, and serve with sliced green onion as a garnish.

Notes

The thickest part of the eggplant will yield the best slices for this recipe. Feel free to save any additional eggplant for another recipe. Alternatively, you can grill the entire eggplant, and enjoy the remaining slices without the egg-filled center. For those without a grill, you can also broil the eggplant.

Beef bacon and eggs

Imagine, if you will, a marriage between traditional pork bacon and beef jerky. That is the flavor you will taste from beef bacon. If you are a bacon lover, as many are, then we encourage you to try beef bacon. It is a delicious way to bring slightly new flavors to a classic breakfast.

Ingredients

- 4 strips beef bacon
- 2 tsp coconut oil
- 1-2 cups shredded green cabbage
- Salt and pepper to taste
- 2-4 eggs

Difficulty:

Prep Time: 10 min

Cook Time: 15 min

Serves: 2

Process

1. Preheat oven to broil at 500°F, and raise the oven rack to the top level.
2. Place beef bacon strips on a baking sheet and set aside.
3. Heat 1 teaspoon coconut oil in a frying pan on medium heat.
4. Sauté green cabbage until soft and a bit crispy. Season with salt and pepper and remove from heat.
5. Heat remaining teaspoon of coconut oil in frying pan on medium heat.
6. Crack eggs into frying pan and cook 2-3 minutes, flipping once. Remove eggs from heat and plate with the cabbage.
7. Place bacon in oven and broil for 7 minutes a side, flipping once.

Notes

When broiling the bacon, the second side will cook faster than the first. Every oven varies in temperature slightly, so keep an eye on the bacon until your first batch is cooked to perfection.

Breakfast burrito

This breakfast is a great way to make use of leftover taco meat, and a delicious way to spice up your typical breakfast routine. We love the flavors of tacos, and this is one of our favorite ways to enjoy them.

Ingredients

- 1/4 lb ground beef or turkey
- 3 eggs
- 1 tsp coconut oil
- 1/8 cup red onion, julienned
- Cilantro for garnish

Seasoning

- 1 tsp cumin
- 1 tsp onion powder
- 1 tsp garlic powder
- 1 tsp paprika
- Salt and pepper to taste

Difficulty:

Prep Time: 10 min

Cook Time: 10 min

Serves: 1

Process

1. Brown ground beef or turkey in a skillet over medium heat.
2. One the meat is no longer pink, season with cumin, onion powder, garlic powder, paprika, salt, and pepper. Once mixed, set aside.
3. Whisk eggs in a small mixing bowl.
4. Heat coconut oil in a large nonstick skillet over medium-low heat.
5. Pour eggs into skillet, making sure they a spread out in a thin, even layer.
6. Slow cook eggs, without flipping, for 6 minutes.
7. Gently slide eggs onto a plate. Top with the seasoned meat, guacamole, salsa, onion, and garnish with cilantro.

Serve with

- Game day guacamole (pg 88)
- Roasted Roma salsa (pg 90)

Notes

Be sure to thoroughly grease your pan before adding the eggs. We typically spread the coconut oil around with a high heat silicone spatula—making several passes to ensure the oil coats the pan evenly.

Frittata

Combining aspects of an omelet and a quiche, this versatile dish is wonderful with any vegetable pairing. Get creative with this one and explore new flavors to always keep your frittatas interesting.

Ingredients

- 3 asparagus spears, chopped
- 3/4 cup yellow onion, diced
- 1 cup white mushrooms, chopped
- 1 cup packed spinach, chopped
- 1 tbsp coconut oil
- 8 eggs
- 2 strips bacon, cooked and crumbled

Difficulty:

Prep Time: 10 min

Cook Time: 15-20 min

Serves: 4

Process

1. Preheat oven to bake at 350° F.
2. In an oven-safe skillet, heat 1/2 tablespoon coconut oil over medium heat.
3. Sauté vegetables for 3 minutes, until the onion is translucent and the mushrooms have softened.
4. Remove vegetables from heat and set aside.
5. In a medium-sized mixing bowl, whisk eggs.
6. Stir vegetables into the eggs.
7. Heat 1/2 tablespoon coconut oil in the oven-safe skillet over medium-low heat.
8. Pour frittata mixture into the skillet and slow cook for 4-5 minutes.
9. Transfer frittata to the oven and cook for 12 minutes, or until the frittata has achieved a spongy firmness to the touch.
10. Slice and serve with crumbled bacon on top, along with a dash of cracked pepper.

Notes

Great mix-ins for frittatas are ground beef or breakfast sausage. You could also add the bacon into the mixture before cooking.

Eggs paleo

This breakfast is our version of eggs Benedict. In place of the traditional hollandaise sauce, we serve ours with an avocado drizzle that reinvents this dish with a primal spin.

Ingredients

- 2 strips bacon
- 1 large slice of tomato
- 1/2 avocado
- Juice of 1/2 lemon
- 1 clove garlic
- 3 tbsp water
- 1 egg
- Pepper to taste

Difficulty: / / /

Prep Time: 10 min

Cook Time: 20 min

Serves: 1

Process

1. Cook bacon over medium heat, allow to cool, then crumble; set aside.
2. Rinse tomato under cold water, and slice into 1/4-inch-thick pieces.
3. Place the meat of 1/2 avocado in a food processor. Add the lemon juice, 1 clove of garlic, and 3 tablespoons of water.
4. Blend until the avocado drizzle is a smooth consistency.
5. Place an egg poacher in a frying pan over medium heat. Crack an egg into the poacher, pour 1/4 cup of water in the frying pan, and cook covered for 4-6 minutes.
6. Plate dish by stacking the egg on the tomato slice. Liberally dress with the avocado drizzle, then sprinkle with cracked pepper and crumbled bacon.

Notes

Although there are many ways to poach an egg, the method is always an egg cooked in nearly boiling water. If you do not have an egg poacher, you can steam your egg by simmering 1/2 cup of water in a frying pan, cracking an egg into it, and covering the pan with a lid. Allow the egg to steam until the yolk turns slightly pink in color.

Kitchen sink omelet

This breakfast is an example of how to use leftover meat, vegetables, and sauces that you have on hand. Everything goes into this omelet, except the kitchen sink!

Ingredients

- 2 tsp coconut oil
- 1/2 cup broccoli, chopped
- 1/3 cup onion, diced
- 2/3 cup ground meat
- 3-4 eggs

Difficulty:

Prep Time: 10 min

Cook Time: 15 min

Serves: 1

Process

1. Heat 1 teaspoon coconut oil in a nonstick skillet over medium heat.
2. Sauté broccoli and onions until tender (about 3 minutes), then set aside.
3. Cook ground meat until no longer pink, and set aside.
4. Clean the skillet, add the remaining 1 tsp of coconut oil, and put the skillet back over the heat.
5. Mix 3-4 eggs in a bowl until yolks and whites are combined, then pour into the freshly oiled, medium-hot skillet. Make sure eggs are evenly distributed.
6. Allow eggs to cook for 1 minute.
7. Pour the cooked ground meat, broccoli, and onions over half of the eggs.
8. Fold the half of the eggs without toppings over the top. Allow to cook for an additional minute or two.
9. Flip the omelet by using two spatulas (or forks), or a bold flick of the wrist.
10. Allow to cook for another 3-4 minutes, then remove from heat and serve.
11. Top with slices of avocado, some salsa, and some of our chimichurri (pg 308) if you have it on hand.

Notes

This omelet is a good way to use leftovers that might otherwise be wasted. Other options to add in are steak, chicken, lamb, pork, or additional veggies of your choice.

Egg bake casserole

This delicious breakfast is a creative way to enjoy having a single-serving egg quiche all to yourself. We love how the top gets crispy while the vegetables in the center are encapsulated in warm, fluffy eggs.

Ingredients

- 2 eggs
- 2 broccoli florets, chopped
- 1/8 cup zucchini, halved and sliced
- 1/8 cup onion, diced
- 2 leaves spinach, chopped
- Pinch of salt
- 1 tsp coconut oil

Difficulty:

Prep Time: 5 min

Cook Time: 20-25 min

Serves: 1

Process

1. Preheat oven to 350°F.
2. Whisk two eggs in a mixing bowl.
3. Stir in chopped vegetables and sprinkle in salt.
4. Lightly grease a single-serving nonstick soufflé dish with the coconut oil.
5. Pour egg mixture into the soufflé dish.
6. Bake at 350°F for 20-25 minutes.

Notes

A side of fresh fruit, bacon, or sausage will go well with this recipe. You can even get creative and mix cooked sausage or ground meat into the eggs prior to cooking, or top with crumbled bacon.

Veggie scramble

This breakfast is the very first that we shared together. This breakfast brings back memories of warm, sunny mornings at the beach after a trip to the local farmers market, enjoyed with a hot cup of coffee.

Ingredients

- 1/2 tbsp coconut oil
- 1/2 cup broccoli, chopped
- 1/2 small onion, diced
- 1/4 medium green pepper, diced
- 2-4 eggs
- Diced avocado and cherry tomatoes for garnish

Difficulty:

Prep Time: 10 min

Cook Time: 4-6 min

Serves: 1-2

Process

1. Heat 1/2 tablespoon of coconut oil in a frying pan over medium heat.
2. Sauté the vegetables for 3 minutes, or until tender.
3. In a small mixing bowl, whisk eggs.
4. Pour the eggs over the vegetables and stir.
5. Stir frequently to scrape the eggs from the frying pan, thus "scrambling" them.
6. Season with a dash of salt and pepper, top with diced tomato and avocado.

Notes

Scrambled eggs go well with a variety of side dishes. You can pair this dish with turkey sausage, bacon, steak, or virtually any animal protein.

Root vegetable hash and poached egg

A simple hash made from root vegetables, brings wonderful color and flavor to your plate in the morning. Warm, crispy flavors of roasted root vegetables pair beautifully with eggs, but would make a great side dish to any meal.

Ingredients

- 1 large beet (1 cup, chopped)
- 3 small turnips (1 cup chopped)
- 1 Vidalia onion (1 cup chopped)
- 2 tbsp extra-virgin olive oil
- Salt and pepper, to taste
- 1 tbsp rosemary, minced
- 1 tbsp garlic, minced
- 1 tsp coconut oil
- 2-4 eggs

Difficulty:

Prep Time: 10 min

Cook Time: 30 min

Serves: 2-4

Process

1. Preheat oven to roast at 400°F.
2. Rinse root vegetables, and chop into bite-sized pieces.
3. Toss vegetables with 2 tablespoons olive oil.
4. Evenly spread vegetables onto a large baking sheet.
5. Season with salt, pepper, and minced rosemary.
6. Roast for 20 minutes, then add minced garlic, stir, and roast for an additional 10 minutes.
7. Root vegetables will be finished when they are crispy around the edges.
8. Heat 1 teaspoon of coconut oil in a nonstick skillet over medium heat.
9. Crack egg into skillet and cook for 30 seconds.
10. Pour 1/4 cup water into the frying pan and cover with lid.
11. Steam the egg until it is fully cooked (the yolk of the egg should have a hint of pink on the top, and none of the white should be translucent).
12. Serve eggs over the root vegetable hash.

Notes

Make sure to thoroughly clean your root vegetables. Beets, especially, tend to hold a lot of dirt, so we will often scrub them clean before cooking. An additional treat with this breakfast would be to serve it with a few slices of bacon.

Coconut-nested eggs

We love making easy meals that look and taste gourmet, especially for breakfast. This dish is no exception! It delivers on flash and flavor, but is a breeze to "whip" up.

Ingredients

- 2 eggs, separated
- 1/4 cup shredded, unsweetened coconut

Difficulty:

Prep Time: 10 min

Cook Time: 10 min

Serves: 1

Process

1. Preheat oven to 350°F.
2. Separate whites and yolks, placing yolks in individual small mixing bowls.
3. Beat egg whites until they are stiff.
4. Fold in the shredded coconut.
5. Shape the egg whites into nests on a parchment-lined baking sheet.
6. Sprinkle a little shredded coconut on top of the nests.
7. Pour yolks into the center of the nests.
8. Bake at 350°F for 10 minutes, until the nests set and the peaks begin to lightly brown.
9. Sprinkle lightly with sea salt, and serve.

Egg muffins

Anyone on the go will appreciate the simplicity of this recipe. These delicious little quiche-like muffins are easy to make ahead of time and grab at a moment's notice.

Ingredients

- 1/2 tsp coconut oil
- 1/2 medium onion, chopped
- 1 cup broccoli, chopped
- 1/4 green pepper, chopped
- 1/4 red pepper, chopped
- 8 eggs
- Salt and pepper to taste

Difficulty:

Prep Time: 10 min

Cook Time: 18-20 min

Makes: 4 large muffins or
        8 small muffins

Process

1. Preheat oven to 400°F.
2. Grease the muffin tin with coconut oil.
3. Rinse and chop all vegetables into 1/4-inch pieces.
4. Divide vegetables evenly between muffin tins.
5. Whisk the eggs, then pour into the tins, dividing it evenly.
6. Sprinkle with salt and pepper, then stir the vegetable and egg mixture briefly to evenly disperse the vegetables throughout the egg.
7. Bake the egg muffins in the oven for 18-20 minutes.

Notes

For best results, thoroughly grease your muffin tin, or use silicone muffin molds. These egg muffins can be made ahead of time, and refrigerated for up to 4 days.

Scrambled eggs with lox and capers

Growing up, my family would often serve lox with bagels and cream cheese at family brunches. This was always a special occasion when family came into town. In my mind, I can still taste the flavors of a toasted bagel topped with cream cheese, lox, red onion, tomato, and capers. For our version of this dish, we replaced the bagel and cream cheese with eggs for an equally delicious and much healthier version.

—Hayley

Ingredients

- 1 tsp coconut oil
- 1/4 cup red onion, chopped
- 3 eggs
- 2 oz smoked salmon ("lox"), chopped
- 1 vine-ripened tomato, sliced
- 1 tsp capers
- 1 tsp chopped parsley
- Black pepper to taste

Difficulty:

Prep Time: 10 min

Cook Time: 8 min

Serves: 1

Process

1. Heat coconut oil in a frying pan over medium heat.
2. Sauté onion until soft in coconut oil.
3. Whisk 3 eggs in small mixing bowl.
4. Mix chopped salmon in with whisked eggs.
5. Pour eggs and salmon over sautéed onion.
6. Cook, stirring gently to scramble.
7. Serve over sliced tomato, and garnish with capers, parsley, and black pepper.

Notes

Be sure to read the label when purchasing smoked salmon. You will want to look for a wild-caught cut without any added sugars.

Steak and eggs with sautéed cabbage

While leftovers are a rare occurrence in our house, we do love utilizing them for breakfast the next morning when we have them. Here is a great way to make use of leftover steak, or a great excuse to throw an extra steak on the grill next time you're cooking out!

Ingredients

- 1.5 cups cabbage
- 1.5 tbsp coconut oil
- Salt and pepper to taste
- 1 egg
- 1/4 lb steak
- 1 tsp parsley, chopped

Difficulty:

Prep Time: 5 min

Cook Time: 15 min

Serves: 1

Process

1. Slice cabbage thinly and rinse with cold water.
2. Preheat skillet to medium-high heat with 1 tablespoon coconut oil.
3. Add cabbage to skillet and season with salt and pepper. Sauté cabbage for 5 minutes; set aside.
4. Add 1/2 tablespoon coconut oil to the skillet, and cook egg on medium-low heat. Cover with a lid and cook for 4-5 minutes.
5. Cut steak into 1/4-inch-thick strips and warm in a frying pan over medium heat.
6. Plate egg and steak over cabbage, top with parsley, and serve.

Notes

For the perfect sunny-side-up egg, cook the egg on medium-low heat slowly, allowing the egg to cook through without flipping. If you do not have leftover steak, this dish would also be great with ground beef.

Huevos rancheros

A popular breakfast throughout the Americas, huevos rancheros is typically served atop a corn or flour tortilla and with refried beans. We make it paleo by ditching those parts, and just adding more of the good stuff!

Ingredients

- 1 tbsp coconut oil
- 2 cloves garlic, minced
- 1 orange bell pepper, chopped
- 1/2 onion, chopped
- 1 jalapeño pepper, minced
- 2 vine-ripened tomatoes, diced
- 1 tsp coconut oil
- 2 eggs
- Cilantro and avocado slices for garnish

Difficulty:

Prep Time: 15 min

Cook Time: 15 min

Serves: 1

Process

1. Heat 1 tablespoon coconut oil in a skillet over medium heat.
2. Sauté garlic, bell pepper, onion, and jalapeño for 3 minutes, or until the onion is translucent and the peppers have softened slightly.
3. Add in diced tomatoes and sauté for 5 minutes; set aside.
4. Heat 1 teaspoon of coconut oil in a nonstick skillet over medium-low heat.
5. Slow-cook two eggs for approximately 6 minutes, until the whites cook through.
6. Plate the eggs topped with the salsa, and garnish with cilantro and avocado slices.

Notes

Be cautious when cooking with jalapeño peppers. Most of the heat lies in the seeds, so for a milder dish, discard the seeds. Make sure to thoroughly wash your hands after handling the peppers, before touching your face or eyes. For extra caution, you can wear rubber gloves.

Slow-cooked steak and eggs

Some days (okay, most days) we just want something simple for breakfast. This one is really easy to prepare, especially when you already have some slow-cooked steak (or pulled pork) on hand. For a little kick, try drizzling your eggs with a bit of Tabasco sauce.

Ingredients

- 1 tbsp beef tallow
- 1/3 lb cooked, shredded beef or pork
- 1 tsp each of: cumin, salt, pepper, smoked paprika, cayenne
- 1/2 tbsp coconut oil
- 2 eggs
- Arugula for garnish
- 10 drops of Tabasco sauce (optional)

Difficulty:

Prep Time: 5 min

Cook Time: 15 min

Serves: 1

Process

1. Heat 1 tablespoon of beef tallow in a skillet over medium heat.
2. Place shredded beef into skillet, and stir in spices until evenly distributed.
3. In a separate nonstick skillet, heat 1/2 tbsp of coconut oil over medium heat
4. Place an egg poacher in the skillet, and crack an egg into it. Repeat with the second egg, or cook both at once if you have enough room in the skillet.
5. Add approximately 1/2 cup of water to the frying pan and cover it with a lid.
6. Cook egg for 5 minutes on medium heat until the top of the egg has cooked.
7. Carefully release the egg from the egg poacher.
8. Place beef on plate, top with the poached eggs, and garnish with some arugula.
9. Drizzle it all with Tabasco sauce if you want an extra kick, and serve.

French omelet

A classic French omelet is fried in butter, and served slightly undercooked, often filled with cheese. Our version, simply seasoned with fresh herbs and filled with ham, is a tasty way to bring a bit of French cooking into your home.

Ingredients

- 1 tbsp rosemary
- 1 tbsp thyme
- 3-4 eggs
- 2 tsp pasture butter
- Salt and pepper to taste
- 1/4 cup of sliced ham

Difficulty:

Prep Time: 5 min

Cook Time: 5 min

Serves: 1

Process

1. Mince rosemary and chop thyme; set aside.
2. Heat a nonstick (or well-oiled) skillet over medium heat.
3. Whisk eggs in a bowl, and set aside.
4. Add butter to skillet. Once melted, add eggs immediately.
5. Sprinkle rosemary and thyme over eggs, add salt and pepper to taste.
6. After 1-2 minutes, add ham to center of the eggs.
7. Once the edges begin to cook, fold each edge inward toward the center. Cook until desired firmness is achieved.
8. Serve with a few slivers of ham on top, garnished with extra sprigs of rosemary and thyme.

Notes

A classic French omelet is served slightly undercooked. You may cook this omelet to your own liking.

Breakfast sausages

Breakfast sausage patties are quite simple to create at home. We love the addition of sausage to our breakfast plate, and with this quick recipe, we can have all the flavors of sausage in the morning, without any unfavorable ingredients.

Ingredients

- 1 lb ground pork
- 1 tsp garlic
- 1 tsp paprika
- 1/2 tsp sage
- 1 tsp fennel seeds
- 1/4 tsp cayenne
- 1/4 tsp white pepper
- 1/2 tsp salt
- 1/2 tsp black pepper
- 2 tbsp coconut oil

Difficulty:

Prep Time: 10 min

Cook Time: 10 min

Serves: 4

Process

1. Combine pork, garlic, and all spices in a mixing bowl, mixing until it reaches an even consistency.
2. Form pork mixture into 2-ounce patties (approximately 8 patties).
3. Heat a skillet to medium heat with 1 tablespoon of coconut oil per 4 patties.
4. Cook the patties for approximately 3-4 minutes per side. Each side should be golden, and the center of the patties should no longer be pink.

Grain-free granola

Our version of granola combines dehydrated nuts, coconut, and fruit. This is our primal version of a breakfast cereal, and also makes for a great snack when you're on the go.

Ingredients

- 1 cup raw sunflower seeds
- 1 cup raw pecans
- 1 cup raw walnuts
- 1 cup raw pumpkin seeds
- 1 cup raw sliced almonds
- 1 cup shredded unsweetened coconut
- 1 cup chopped medjool dates
- 1 cup raisins

Difficulty:

Prep Time: 10-12 hrs

Cook Time: 10-12 hrs

Serves: 10

Process

1. Soak nuts and seeds in warm water and a tablespoon of salt overnight for 10-12 hours.
2. Drain and spread onto a baking sheet.
3. Set oven temperature at 110°F, and dehydrate for 10-12 hours (if your lowest oven setting is higher than 110°F, leave the oven door slightly ajar).
4. Coarsely chop dehydrated nuts and place in a large bowl.
5. Mix in shredded coconut, chopped dates, and raisins.
6. Toss lightly to evenly distribute all ingredients.
7. Serve granola with unsweetened almond milk, or coconut milk.
8. Store any excess in an airtight container.

Notes

This recipe can be scaled to any size you desire. However, if you're taking the time to do this, you might as well make more rather than less. You may also prefer to split the batch in half to use half for granola and half just for snacking or another future recipe.

Coconut flour waffles and pancakes

The warm, sweet flavors of waffles make us think of lazy weekend mornings, enjoying a big breakfast with loved ones. This breakfast is an indulgence that we don't enjoy too often, but it is great for a special occasion.

Ingredients

- 1/4 cup coconut flour
- 4 eggs
- 1 tbsp coconut milk
- 1 tbsp cinnamon
- 1/4 tsp nutmeg
- 1/4 tsp baking soda
- 1 tsp pure maple syrup (optional)

Banana nut topping

- 1 tsp coconut oil
- 1 banana
- 1/4 cup pecans, chopped

Difficulty: / / /

Prep Time: 20 min

Cook Time: 10 min

Serves: 2

Process

1. In a medium-sized mixing bowl, blend all ingredients with a hand mixer.
2. Heat waffle iron to "waffle" setting—typically medium-high heat.
3. Drop batter into center of waffle iron to cover about 3/4 of area. This batter does not expand the way traditional flour waffles do.
4. Waffles are done when they easily separate from the waffle iron, typically 3-5 minutes.

For the topping

1. Heat coconut oil in a nonstick frying pan on medium heat.
2. Slice banana and add to frying pan.
3. Sear banana slices until brown and crispy on the bottom side, then flip.
4. Add pecans to frying pan and lightly toast with the seared banana slices.
5. Top over waffles or pancakes and serve.

Notes

To make pancakes, use 1/4 teaspoon cinnamon instead of 1 tablespoon. In a medium-sized mixing bowl, blend all ingredients with a hand mixer. Heat coconut oil in a nonstick frying pan or griddle to medium heat. Pour 1/8 cup of batter into frying pan or griddle. Cook for 2 minutes, flip, then cook for 2 more minutes. Repeat with the remaining batter.

Almond milk

Ingredients

- 1 lb raw almonds
- 4 cups purified water

Difficulty:
Prep Time: 8 hrs
Makes: 4 cups

Process

1. Soak raw almonds in water for a minimum of 8 hours.
2. Drain water from almonds and rinse thoroughly.
3. Place almonds in a food processor or high-speed blender along with 4 cups of water.
4. Blend nuts and water until smooth.
5. Pour liquid into a large bowl through a clean paint strainer bag.
6. Gently squeeze the pulp in the paint strainer bag to wring out the remaining almond milk.
7. Serve or keep refrigerated in a glass container.

Coconut milk

Ingredients

- Meat of 1 coconut
- Purified water

Difficulty:
Prep Time: 15 min
Makes: 3-4 cups

Process

1. Crack coconut over a large bowl or sink by striking it around its equator with the back side of a large knife or cleaver. Continue striking and rotating until the coconut cracks open.
2. Separate coconut meat from shell, and remove the skin with a vegetable peeler or knife.
3. Cut coconut into 1/2-inch chunks, and add to a high-speed blender or food processor. Cover with purified water, and blend until smooth.
4. Pour pureed coconut through a clean paint strainer bag, and gently squeeze to wring all coconut milk out.
5. Serve or keep refrigerated in a glass container.

Appetizers

When transitioning to a grain-free lifestyle, the idea of serving guests can be intimidating. In this section we have created numerous appetizers that will be sure to impress your friends. Here, we provide you with recipes for any celebration, be it a holiday, birthday, or just a fun gathering. Laugh, love, eat, and enjoy!

Game day guacamole

Guacamole is a party-time staple for us. Always a hit, this creamy dip pairs beautifully with most vegetables. Whether it is a summer cookout or Monday night football, we are always sure to serve up some delicious guac` and fresh veggies for dipping.

Ingredients

- 2 ripe avocados
- 1 medium Roma tomato, seeded and diced
- 1/2 red onion, diced
- 2 tbsp cilantro, chopped
- 2-3 cloves garlic
- Juice of 1/2 lime
- 1 tsp salt, or to taste

Difficulty:
Prep Time: 10 minutes
Serves: 4-8

Process

1. Split avocados in half, discard pits, and scoop the flesh out with a spoon into a medium-sized mixing bowl.
2. Mash avocados with a fork until creamy with small chunks.
3. Add in tomatoes, onion, and cilantro.
4. Press garlic cloves over bowl, and add lime juice. Mix together, until all is combined evenly.
5. Add salt to taste.
6. Garnish with cilantro and lime slices.

Serve with

- Endive spears or fresh-cut vegetables

Notes

Avocado will turn brown (oxidize) if exposed to air for more than 30 minutes. If you are preparing this guacamole in advance for a party, add the lime juice called for in the recipe, if nothing else, to slow the oxidation of the avocado.

Roasted Roma salsa

You don't need tortilla chips to enjoy great salsa. We ditch the chips in favor of some fresh-cut vegetables. Carrots, celery, endive, broccoli, bell peppers—they are all great companions to fresh salsa.

Ingredients

- 1/2 medium yellow onion
- 1/2 medium red bell pepper, sliced
- 1/4 jalapeño pepper
- 2 cloves garlic, chopped
- 1.25 cups organic fire-roasted, canned diced tomatoes (no salt added, do not drain)
- Juice of 1 lime
- Salt and pepper to taste
- 1/4 cup cilantro

Difficulty:

Prep Time: 10 min

Serves: 4-8

Process

1. In a food processor or high-speed blender, pulse onion to chop.
2. Add in red bell pepper, jalapeño pepper, and garlic. Continue to pulse until all are diced.
3. Add in diced tomatoes, lime juice, salt and pepper, and cilantro. Continue to pulse until all is blended.
4. Serve garnished with lime wedges and a few cilantro leaves.

Notes

Want to make your salsa a little more caliente? (That's hot, for all the non-Spanish-speakers out there). Just add some more jalapeño. If you're bold, you can add some of the seeds too.

Hot pepper hummus

One of my favorite non-paleo blogs to visit is Not Without Salt. I love the food photography inspiration, and the name is just so catchy. If my mom were to start blogging, hers might be called Not Without Hummus. We love this versatile veggie dip too, though our version is made primarily from zucchini and not chick peas. You'll love it!

—Bill

Ingredients

- 2 medium zucchini
- 3/4 cup tahini
- 1/4 cup extra-virgin olive oil
- 1/2 cup lemon juice
- 2 large cloves garlic, minced
- 1/2 tbsp ground cumin
- 2 tsp salt

Garnish

- 1/4 cup red peppers, finely chopped
- 1/4 cup green peppers, finely chopped
- 1/4 tsp red pepper flakes
- 1 tbsp extra-virgin olive oil
- Salt and pepper to taste
- 2 tbsp pine nuts

Difficulty:

Prep Time: 20 min

Serves: 6–8

Process

1. Peel and chop zucchini.
2. Place chopped zucchini in food processor, and pulse.
3. Add in tahini, olive oil, and fresh lemon juice, and pulse again.
4. Add garlic, cumin, and salt, and blend until smooth.

For the garnish

1. Sauté chopped peppers and red pepper flakes in olive oil until tender. Add salt and pepper.
2. In a small sauce pan over low heat, lightly toast pine nuts.
3. Garnish the hummus with the spicy peppers and pine nuts.
4. Serve with fresh vegetables.

Baba ghanoush

Ingredients

- 1 eggplant
- 1/4 cup tahini
- Juice of 1 lemon
- 1 tsp each of salt and pepper
- 2 tbsp extra-virgin olive oil

Difficulty:

Prep Time: 5 min

Serves: 3-6

Process

1. Prick the eggplant on all sides with a fork, and place on a baking sheet.
2. Roast eggplant in 400°F oven for 30 minutes.
3. Place eggplant in large bowl of cold water for approximately 5 minutes.
4. Peel skin from eggplant and discard. Chop eggplant into large chunks.
5. Place eggplant chunks in a high speed blender or food processor along with tahini, lemon juice, salt, pepper, and olive oil.
6. Blend until smooth.

Herb crackers

Ingredients

- 2 cups almond flour
- 1 cup flax meal
- 2 tsp each: cumin, garlic, onion powder, oregano, black pepper, and salt
- 2 eggs
- 2 tbsp extra-virgin olive oil

Difficulty:

Prep Time: 5 min

Cook Time: 15 min

Serves: 3-6

Process

1. Preheat oven to 350°F.
2. In a large mixing bowl, combine almond flour, flax meal, and spices.
3. Whisk eggs and pour over flour mixture.
4. Add in olive oil. Stir all ingredients together until it forms a dough.
5. Roll dough into a large ball, and place on a parchment-lined baking sheet.
6. Cover dough with another sheet of parchment paper. Using a rolling pin, roll out into a 1/4-inch-thick layer.
7. Score dough with a knife to desired cracker size.
8. Bake crackers for 15 minutes.
9. Let cool, break crackers into squares, and serve.

Grilled olives

In the belief that almost everything tastes better grilled, we like to take a handful of mixed olives tossed with herbs and throw them over some hot coals. The result is a delectable appetizer with smoky, complex flavors, and minimal effort.

Ingredients

- 1 cup mixed, whole olives
- 1 tbsp rosemary, minced
- 1 tbsp thyme, minced
- 2 cloves garlic, minced
- Black pepper to taste

Difficulty:

Prep Time: 3 min

Cook Time: 6-8 min

Serves: 4

Process

1. Preheat grill to medium-high heat.
2. Toss the olives with the herbs to evenly coat. If olives are not already packed in olive oil, add 1 teaspoon of olive oil to help the herbs adhere to the olives.
3. Grill olives in a grill basket for 6-8 minutes over medium-high heat, rolling frequently to evenly cook olives.
4. Olives will be done when they have slight grill marks on them, and begin to soften.

Fried green tomatoes

Ever since watching the movie Fried Green Tomatoes with my mom years ago, I always wanted to try the actual recipe. Our version uses a light dredging of coconut flour, and is then fried in bacon grease. The chopped bacon on top is really what makes this dish a hit!

—Hayley

Ingredients

- 3 strips bacon
- 2 green tomatoes
- 2 eggs
- 1/4 cup coconut flour
- Salt and pepper to taste

Difficulty:

Prep Time: 8 min

Cook Time: 12-15 min

Serves: 4-8

Process

1. Cook bacon over medium heat, allow to cool, then crumble. Reserve bacon grease for cooking tomatoes.
2. Clean tomatoes, and slice into 1/8-inch-thick pieces.
3. Whip the eggs in a shallow dish.
4. Dip tomato slices in egg wash, then dredge in coconut flour.
5. Sauté tomato slices in bacon fat for 2-3 minutes per side over medium heat.
6. Remove from heat, sprinkle with salt and pepper.
7. Serve with crumbled bacon.

Notes

Cooking time will vary depending on your stove temperature and the tomato thickness. It is usually best to do a "test" piece with one slice of tomato to gauge adjustments.

Prosciutto e melone

This classic Italian appetizer plays the complimentary tastes of salty and sweet off of one another. In our version, we weave the prosciutto through the skewer of cantaloupe so that the flavor pairing is enjoyed in every bite.

Ingredients

- 1/2 small cantaloupe
- 1/4 lb prosciutto crudo

Difficulty:

Prep Time: 10 min

Serves: 6-10

Process

1. Cut cantaloupe in half, and scoop out small balls with a melon baller or rounded measuring spoon.
2. Cut prosciutto into 1/2-inch strips, approximately 6 inches long.
3. Weave prosciutto ribbon through a stack of three melon balls, and skewer with a toothpick.

Notes

Choosing a perfectly ripe cantaloupe is easy. To start, smell the cantaloupe. It should have a sweet scent, and smell just like the inner fruit of the melon. If the skin has an orange tint to it, it is ripe. If it appears green underneath, it may not be ripe yet. A soft cantaloupe is overripe and should not be selected.

Pan-seared artichoke hearts

The heart of the artichoke is like the pot of gold at the end of the rainbow—it is truly a treat! Artichoke hearts, commonly found canned in stores, are tasty. However, they cannot compare to the fabulous taste of freshly steamed artichoke hearts. For this recipe, the hearts are the star of the show. This dish brings a bit of gourmet to a beloved vegetable of ours.

Ingredients

- 2 artichokes, leaves removed
- 1 tbsp coconut oil

Difficulty:

Prep Time: 5 min

Cook Time: 15-20 min

Serves: 2

Process

1. Carefully trim the sharp tips from the leaves of the artichoke.
2. Cut the outer leaves off of the artichoke until you have almost reached the choke and heart.
3. Fill a large soup pot with water. Place the artichokes into the water, and bring to a boil over medium-high heat.
4. Boil hearts for 10 minutes, or until you can easily slide a fork into the stem.
5. Remove hearts from water and allow to cool.
6. Cut the choke out, as well as any remaining leaves.
7. Slice the heart into 1/2-inch pieces.
8. Sear slices in a frying pan with coconut oil over medium-high heat.

Serve with

- Garlic and rosemary aioli (pg 322)

Notes

The "choke" of the artichoke is the fuzzy center that covers the heart. This part of the vegetable is not edible, and should always be removed before consuming.

Deviled eggs

Deviled eggs are a simple appetizer that are often served at parties. For our version, we make these paleo by the use of our homemade mayo. The perfect finger food for a gathering of friends, or when joined by a side of veggies and fruit, they can also be a quick meal.

Ingredients

- 6-8 eggs
- 2 tbsp mayonnaise (pg 312)
- Salt and pepper to taste
- Paprika for garnish

Difficulty:

Prep Time: 10 min

Cook Time: 10 min

Serves: 3-4

Process

1. Place eggs in a pot and cover with water. Bring water to a boil. Boil eggs for 10 minutes. Rinse under cold water. Peel when cooled.
2. Slice eggs, lengthwise, down the center.
3. Remove yolk and place in a bowl.
4. Mix yolks with mayonnaise, salt, and pepper.
5. Scoop yolk mixture back into the hard-boiled egg whites.
6. Sprinkle with paprika and serve.

Spicy sautéed calamari

Calamari is often served deep fried here in the United States. Though it has a unique texture (somewhat similar to al dente linguine), the light flavor is delightful and worth trying. We love ours with the zing of red pepper flakes and a hint of fish sauce.

Ingredients

- 1 tsp coconut oil
- 3 cloves garlic, minced
- 1 lb calamari rings
- 1 tsp coconut aminos
- 2 drops fish sauce
- Salt and white pepper to taste
- 1/2 tsp red pepper flakes

Difficulty:

Prep Time: 10 min

Cook Time: 5-6 min

Serves: 4-8

Process

1. Heat oil in frying pan over medium heat.
2. Add garlic to oil and sauté for 1 minute.
3. Add calamari and continue to sauté for 1 minute.
4. Add coconut aminos, fish sauce, salt and pepper, and red pepper flakes. Sauté for an additional 3 minutes, until the calamari is opaque and the sides begin to curl inward.

Bacon-wrapped scallops

Our take on this popular appetizer involves the addition of smoked paprika to give great warmth to the flavors of the dish. The crisp bacon nicely compliments the tender scallops, while infusing them with a smoky yet sweet flavor.

Ingredients

- 12-18 medium wild-caught scallops
- 1 lb bacon
- Smoked paprika

Difficulty:

Prep Time: 10 min

Cook Time: 35 min

Serves: 4-8

Process

1. Preheat oven to 425°F.
2. Rinse scallops under cold water.
3. Cut bacon strips in half.
4. Wrap each scallop with 1/2 strip of bacon.
5. Skewer 2-3 bacon-wrapped scallops per skewer.
6. Sprinkle with smoked paprika, seasoning both sides.
7. Bake at 425°F for 20 minutes. Flip, then bake for an additional 15 minutes.

Prosciutto-wrapped asparagus

This appetizer has gained popularity in recent years, and it's obvious why. These clever little wraps have the salty and savory thing going on. They also have quite an appealing look to them, which makes them the perfect precursor to a fancy dinner party.

Ingredients

- 1/3 lb prosciutto, sliced thinly
- 1 lb asparagus
- 1/2 yellow onion, thinly sliced
- Salt to taste

Difficulty:

Prep Time: 15 min

Cook Time: 15-20 min

Serves: 8

Process

1. Rinse and cut asparagus into 4-inch pieces.
2. Preheat oven to 400°F.
3. Place a piece of prosciutto on a plate. Lay 4 asparagus spears and a few slices of onion on top.
4. Roll up the prosciutto around the asparagus and onion.
5. Place rolls in a glass baking dish, and bake at 400°F for 15-20 minutes, or until the prosciutto gets crispy and the asparagus begins to turn golden brown at the tips.

Shrimp cocktail

Shrimp cocktail always brings back memories of warm evenings at the shore, enjoying the company of family and the flavors of fresh seafood. This classic appetizer works well for casual, outdoor gatherings and formal affairs alike.

Ingredients

- 1 lb peeled, tail-on, raw shrimp
- Lime wedges for garnish
- Cocktail sauce (pg 324)

Difficulty:

Prep Time: 5 min

Cook Time: 5-8 min

Serves: 6-8

Process

1. Bring a large soup pot of water to boil over medium-high heat.
2. Drop raw shrimp into boiling water.
3. Cook until the shrimp rise to the surface and turn pink.
4. Drain water from shrimp and rinse under cool water.
5. Keep shrimp cold over ice.
6. Garnish with lime wedges and serve with a side of cocktail sauce.

Oysters Rockefeller

Oysters Rockefeller can be made many ways. Our spin on this mid-Atlantic staple is to keep things simple with a short ingredient list. This dish is exponentially more rewarding if you choose to shuck your own oysters.

Ingredients

- 12 fresh oysters
- 1 tbsp extra-virgin olive oil
- 3 cloves garlic, minced
- 1/2 shallot, minced
- 2.5 packed cups spinach, chopped
- 1 tbsp parsley
- Salt and pepper to taste
- Red pepper flakes to taste

Difficulty:

Prep Time: 20 min

Cook Time: 20-25 min

Serves: 3-6

Process

1. Clean oysters with a stiff-bristle brush under cold water.
2. Shuck oysters according to the instructions in the "Notes" section below.
3. Pour a thin layer of kosher salt on a baking sheet. Place oysters on salted baking sheet.
4. Preheat oven to 400°F.
5. Heat olive oil in a frying pan over medium heat.
6. Sauté garlic and shallot until tender.
7. Add the spinach, parsley, salt, pepper, and red pepper flakes. Continue to sauté until the spinach is wilted.
8. Remove spinach topping from heat and allow to cool.
9. Top each oyster with the spinach mixture.
10. Bake at 400°F for 20 minutes, or until the topping is lightly toasted and the oysters have started to curl.

Notes

Shuck the oysters using a thick gardening glove and a sturdy (but dull) knife. Hold the oyster in the gloved hand with the flatter side up, keeping the oyster as level as possible. Locate the hinge at the 'tip' of the shell, and insert the knife tip to pry the shell apart. Apply twisting pressure to lift the top portion off. Once the shell pops open, keep the oyster flat to prevent the juices inside from dripping out. Discard the top portion of the shell. Use the knife to separate the meat of the oyster from the shell by sliding it under the end opposite the hinge near the curved lip.

Shrimp and bacon squash blossoms

Stuffed squash blossoms are a tasty finger food that will be sure to impress your guests. The lightly wilted blossoms will burst with smoky shrimp flavor with each bite. The crumbled bacon adds the perfect crunch to the soft shrimp, and a hint of cayenne gives this dish just the right kick of heat.

Ingredients

- 1 lb cooked shrimp, diced
- 4 strips bacon, crumbled
- 1 tsp smoked paprika
- 1/2 tsp garlic powder
- 1/4 tsp cayenne pepper
- 1/8 cup (heaping) mayonnaise (pg 312)
- 15-20 zucchini blossoms

Difficulty:

Prep Time: 20 min

Cook Time: 10 min

Serves: 4-8

Process

1. Place shrimp in a large soup pot filled with water, and allow to boil until shrimp are pink and float to the surface of the water.
2. Drain shrimp and allow to cool.
3. Heat a nonstick skillet to medium heat, and fry bacon until crispy. Remove bacon from pan and allow to cool, reserving the bacon grease for frying the stuffed blossoms.
4. Whisk smoked paprika, garlic, and cayenne into the mayonnaise.
5. When cool, dice the shrimp, and place in a medium sized mixing bowl.
6. Crumble the bacon and sprinkle over the diced shrimp.
7. Pour in the smoky mayo, and stir until evenly combined.
8. To prepare the blossoms, rinse the outside, and carefully trim the pistil or stamen from the inside of each blossom.
9. Carefully stuff each blossom with a small spoonful of the shrimp and bacon mixture.
10. Lightly sear each blossom on all sides in the bacon grease until the outsides are lightly wilted.

Notes

Beware of bumble bees and other '"Creepy crawlers" inside freshly picked blossoms! If you cannot get a hold of squash blossoms, an alternative option would be to stuff the shrimp mixture into baby portobello caps and bake them until the mushrooms soften slightly. The shrimp mixture is also delicious to eat on its own.

Buffalo wings

Ingredients

- 2.5 lbs chicken wings
- 1/4 cup coconut oil, melted
- 1 cup buffalo sauce (pg 324)

Difficulty:

Prep Time: 15 min

Cook Time: 50-60 min

Serves: 6

Process

1. Preheat oven to 325°F.
2. Melt 1/4 cup coconut oil, and mix with buffalo sauce.
3. Pour over wings, and toss to coat.
4. Bake at 325°F for 50-60 minutes.

Serve with

- Dill mayonnaise dip (pg 314)

Butter garlic wings

Ingredients

- 1/2 cup unsalted pasture butter
- 10 cloves garlic, minced
- 1 tsp salt
- 2.5 lbs chicken wings

Difficulty:

Prep Time: 15 min

Cook Time: 50-60 min

Serves: 6

Process

1. Heat butter in a small sauce pan over medium-low heat.
2. Add minced garlic to the butter, stirring frequently.
3. Preheat oven to 325°F.
4. Bring butter and garlic to a light boil, then reduce heat and simmer for 3 minutes. Add 1 teaspoon salt.
5. Pour butter-garlic mixture over wings, and toss to coat.
6. Bake wings at 325°F for 50-60 minutes.

Serve with

- Dill mayonnaise dip (pg 314)

Grilled clams with garlic drizzle

Grilled clams are a delicious summer appetizer that any house guest will love. These take only minutes to cook on a hot grill, and topped with a garlic and butter drizzle, they will quickly become a favorite to serve.

Ingredients

- 12-15 small clams
- 3 large cloves garlic, minced
- 1/4 cup unsalted pasture butter
- 1 tbsp parsley, finely minced
- 1 tsp salt

Difficulty:

Prep Time: 5 min

Cook Time: 10 min

Serves: 3-6

Process

1. Rinse and soak clams prior to cooking. Discard any clams that are open prior to cooking.
2. Sauté the minced garlic in the pasture butter until the garlic just slightly browns. Remove from heat.
3. Mince parsley, and mix into the butter and garlic mixture.
4. Preheat grill to medium-high heat.
5. Place clams on grill and cook until they open. Any clams that do not open within a few moments of the others should not be eaten.
6. Drizzle the butter and garlic mixture over the open clams.
7. Sprinkle lightly with fine salt, and serve.

Chorizo poppers

Stuffed miniature bell peppers make the perfect party appetizer. They are bright and colorful, and easy for people to eat while standing. These poppers are just bursting with flavor, and are always a hit, even with the non-paleo crowd.

Ingredients

- 1 lb ground turkey
- 4 cloves garlic, minced
- 2 tbsp chili powder
- 1 tbsp paprika
- 1/2 tbsp oregano
- 1/2 tbsp cumin
- 1 tsp red pepper flakes
- 1/2 tsp salt
- 1 tsp black pepper
- 1 tbsp apple cider vinegar
- 1 lb mini bell peppers
- 1/2 onion, chopped
- 1 large tomato, diced
- 1 tbsp cilantro, minced

Difficulty:

Prep Time: 8-12 hrs

Cook Time: 20-25 min

Serves: 6-8

Process

1. In a medium-sized mixing bowl, season ground turkey with garlic powder, chili powder, paprika, oregano, cumin, red pepper flakes, salt, black pepper, and apple cider vinegar.
2. Combine turkey with chorizo spices until the spices are evenly distributed throughout the ground turkey.
3. Cover mixing bowl with plastic wrap and refrigerate overnight.
4. Preheat oven to 400°F.
5. Rinse mini bell peppers under cool water.
6. Remove tops of peppers, as well as the seeds and membrane from the inside of the peppers, set aside peppers.
7. Remove seasoned ground turkey from refrigerator and brown in a skillet over medium heat.
8. Remove ground turkey from heat, and stir in chopped tomato, onion, and minced cilantro.
9. Stuff mini bell peppers with chorizo turkey mixture, and place on a baking sheet.
10. Bake peppers for 20-25 minutes at 400°F, or until edges are golden and peppers are somewhat soft.
11. Garnish with cilantro and serve.

Entrées

The main course is our favorite part of any meal. We've divided this section into three main categories: meat, poultry, and seafood. Within these three groups, you will find everything from quick and simple weeknight dinners to extravagant entrées fit for foreign dignitaries (or your close friends). No matter whom you are cooking for, these dishes are packed with big flavor that are sure delight your taste buds and impress everyone around the table. So pull up a chair, because we're about to serve the main course!

[Meat]

Skirt steak with chive butter

A simply grilled steak is even more mouth watering with homemade chive pasture butter melting over top of it. This recipe brings a taste of gourmet to your plate with the use of only 4 ingredients!

Ingredients

- 1 lb skirt steak
- Salt to taste
- 3 tbsp unsalted pasture butter, room temperature
- 1/4 tsp salt
- 1 tbsp chopped chives

Difficulty:

Prep Time: 15 min

Cook Time: 6 min

Serves: 2-4

Process

1. Preheat grill to high heat.
2. Rinse skirt steak under cold water, and pat dry with a paper towel.
3. Cut skirt steak into 3 pieces of equal length.
4. Sprinkle each side generously with sea salt.
5. Grill for 3 minutes per side.
6. Remove from grill and allow to rest for 5 minutes.
7. While steak is resting, whisk butter, 1/4 teaspoon salt, and chives with a fork.
8. Slice steak against the grain. Top with chive butter and serve.

Notes

Skirt steak is a very thin and long cut of steak. It is easier to handle when cut into smaller pieces for cooking. It will cook very fast due to how thin it is.

Zucchini lasagne

Our recipe for lasagne avoids conventional wheat-based noodles, using instead some thinly sliced zucchini. This simple substitution makes all the difference in this dish, contributing even more flavor to a favorite of many. For a primal twist, you could even add a little cheese!

Ingredients

- 1 lb ground beef
- 3 cloves garlic, minced
- 1 small onion, chopped
- 1 small green pepper, chopped
- 6 oz tomato paste, no salt added
- 15 oz tomato sauce, no salt added
- 1 tbsp fresh parsley
- 1 tbsp basil
- 1 tbsp oregano
- Salt and pepper to taste
- 1 zucchini, sliced thinly
- 1.25 cups mushrooms, sliced

Difficulty: ///

Prep Time: 10 min

Cook Time: 35-45 min

Serves: 2

Process

1. Brown the ground beef in a large pot over medium heat, stirring frequently.
2. Add in garlic, onion and green pepper, and continue to sauté for 5 minutes.
3. Stir in tomato paste and tomato sauce.
4. Add in parsley, basil, oregano, salt and pepper, continue to stir.
5. Bring sauce to a light boil, then remove from heat.
6. Grease a 9" x 13" baking dish with coconut oil.
7. Place a thin layer (1/2 inch) of the sauce in the baking dish.
8. Layer zucchini and mushrooms over sauce, and repeat, alternating layering of sauce, then zucchini and mushrooms.
9. Bake lasagne at 325°F for 15 minutes, covered with foil.
10. After 15 minutes, remove foil, increase temperature to 350°F, and bake for an additional 15 minutes.

Notes

The zucchini and mushrooms will release water upon cooking, with that in mind, the sauce for this recipe is thicker than would be expected. The addition of a second can of tomato sauce to the recipe is fine if you prefer a sauce that is not as thick.

Leg of lamb

When I was very small, I can remember making roast leg of lamb with my Grandy Kyp. She always included me in the process of cooking, and she taught me along the way. For the reinvention of her recipe, we were lucky to have her join us for the cooking, and the eating!

—Hayley

Ingredients

- 3-4 lb leg of lamb
- 1 fist of garlic, peeled
- 2 tbsp fresh thyme, chopped
- Salt and pepper to taste

Difficulty:

Prep Time: 15 min

Cook Time: 25 min/lb

Total Time: 2-4 hrs

Serves: 4-8

Process

1. Preheat the oven to roast at 325°F.
2. Rinse lamb under cold water, place in a broiler pan, and pat dry with a paper towel.
3. Peel cloves of garlic and carefully prick the lamb with a knife to stud with the cloves of garlic into the meat.
4. In a mortar and pestle, blend thyme, salt, and pepper.
5. Rub thyme, salt, and pepper on the lamb.
6. Roast at 325°F, 25 minutes per pound to yield a medium-rare roast.

Serve with

- Roasted baby carrots (pg 336)

Chinese spiced ribs

No rib recipe would be good enough for our book if it weren't falling-off-the-bone delicious. This is not your typical rib recipe though. A dry rub of exotic spices seasons the pork perfectly, while the sesame ginger glaze brings this dish to smoky, juicy perfection.

Ingredients

- 6 lbs pork baby back ribs
- 1 tbsp Chinese spice blend
- 1 tsp curry powder
- 1/2 tsp paprika
- 1/2 tsp ground coriander

Sesame Ginger Glaze

- 3 tbsp sesame oil
- 1/3 cup coconut aminos
- 1/2 tsp fish sauce
- 2 cloves garlic, minced
- 1 tbsp ginger root, minced

Difficulty: / / /

Prep Time: 1.5 hrs

Cook Time: 35 min

Serves: 6

Process

1. Cut slabs of baby back ribs into 6 rib portions.
2. Fill two large soup pots 2/3 full with water, bring to a low boil, cover and par boil the ribs for 30 minutes.
3. Drain ribs and allow to cool on a baking sheet.
4. Once cool, generously season with Chinese spice blend, curry power, paprika, and ground coriander.
5. Cover with foil and place in the refrigerator for 1 hour.
6. Soak hickory chips in water for 1 hour.
7. Place hickory chips in a smoker box, and place smoker box in grill (see your grill instructions for best placement).
8. Heat grill to low heat.
9. Combine glaze ingredients in a small bowl, and whisk to combine.
10. Grill ribs for 20 minutes.
11. After 20 minutes, baste with glaze and continue to cook over low heat for an additional 15 minutes.

Serve with

- Asian broccoli slaw (pg 272)

Notes

As an alternate take on this recipe, you could skip the spice rub and baste the ribs instead with our barbecue sauce (pg 306).

Beef with broccoli

Growing up, we both enjoyed the flavors of Chinese cuisine. This dish brings all those flavors to life, but with a much healthier approach. Simple, bold flavors will make this dish an instant classic in your house.

Ingredients

- 2 tbsp sesame oil
- 5 cloves garlic, minced
- 2 tbsp ginger, minced
- 1 lb of beef, cut into 1" cubes
- 4 cups broccoli florets
- 1/4 cup green onion, thinly sliced
- 1/4 cup coconut aminos
- 1 tsp each, salt and pepper
- 1 tsp red pepper flakes

Difficulty:

Prep Time: 10 min

Cook Time: 15 min

Serves: 4

Process

1. Heat sesame oil in a wok or skillet over high heat.
2. Add garlic and ginger to wok, and sauté for 2 minutes to infuse the sesame oil with their flavor.
3. Add steak, stirring frequently, until browned on all sides.
4. Once the steak has seared, add in the broccoli and continue to sauté over high heat.
5. Add green onion, and an extra tablespoon of oil if necessary.
6. Pour in coconut aminos, and season with salt, pepper, and red pepper flakes.
7. Continue to sauté for another 2-3 minutes, until all flavors have combined.
8. Garnish with a sprinkling of sesame seeds and serve.

Notes

To complete this dish, serve over cauliflower rice (pg 348) or baked spaghetti squash (pg 348).

Strip steak with chimichurri

Chimichurri is a fresh and slightly spicy sauce that can be used as a garnish over meat, eggs, or fish, as well as a delicious marinade. We enjoy chimichurri drizzled over our steaks or cooked over a fish of our choice.

Ingredients

- 1 cup, packed, flat-leaf parsley
- 3-4 garlic cloves, chopped
- Juice of 2 lemons
- 1/2 cup extra-virgin olive oil
- 1 tsp salt
- 1 tsp ground black pepper
- 1/4 tsp red pepper flakes
- 4 New York strip steaks

Difficulty:
Prep Time: 15 min
Cook Time: 12 min
Serves: 4

Process

1. Thoroughly rinse parsley, and removed leaves from stems.
2. Chop garlic cloves and set aside.
3. Slice lemons and discard seeds.
4. In a food processor, blend parsley, olive oil, lemon juice, and garlic.
5. Pour into a small mixing bowl and add salt, pepper, and red pepper flakes.
6. Preheat grill to high heat.
7. Lightly season steaks with sea salt on both sides.
8. Grill steaks for approximately 6 minutes per side, flipping once.
9. Drizzle chimichurri over steaks and serve.

Notes

Chimichurri makes a great marinade for fish, chicken, or steak. We have enjoyed chimichurri both ways, and we highly recommend giving a few options a shot. One batch makes more than enough to try it out with a few recipes!

Beef tenderloin with balsamic drizzle

Best served rare to medium rare, beef tenderloin is one of the most prized cuts of the cow. Our favorite way of preparing beef tenderloin is to sear it with a tangy mustard-based crust and serve it over asparagus and mint with a balsamic drizzle. Divine would be an understatement.

Ingredients

- 1.5 lb beef tenderloin tip
- 1 tbsp Dijon mustard
- 1 tsp each of: ground ginger, garlic powder, onion powder, cumin, coriander, salt, pepper
- 2 tbsp olive oil (for searing)
- 1 lb asparagus, tough ends removed, chopped into 2" pieces

Garnish

- 1/4 cup fresh cilantro
- 6 fresh mint leaves, julienned
- 1 green onion, diagonally sliced
- 1 tbsp extra-virgin olive oil
- 1 tbsp balsamic vinegar

Difficulty:

Prep Time: 15 min

Cook Time: 20-30 min

Serves: 4

Process

1. Allow beef to come to room temperature for 30 minutes prior to cooking.
2. Brush all sides of beef with 1 tablespoon of mustard, until evenly coated.
3. Roll beef in spices, and press lightly to evenly coat.
4. Heat olive oil in skillet over high heat.
5. Sear on high for 6-7 minutes, turning to sear all sides evenly. This will yield rare beef. For medium-rare, place in 400°F oven for an additional 5-10 minutes.
6. Let beef rest for 5 minutes before carving.
7. While beef is resting, blanch the asparagus.
8. Bring a pot of water to a rolling boil, add the trimmed asparagus and allow to cook for 2-5 minutes. Pour asparagus into a metal strainer and place into an ice water bath. Set aside to cool.
9. Thinly slice beef against grain.
10. Plate over asparagus, and garnish with cilantro, mint, and green onion.
11. Drizzle with olive oil and balsamic vinegar, serve.

Grilled lamb chops

Lamb chops are a tasty way to bring new flavors to summer time grilling. For this recipe we use a simple seasoning of lemon, garlic, shallot, and oregano to enhance the wonderful flavor of the juicy lamb chops.

Ingredients

- 1/4 cup extra-virgin olive oil
- Juice of 1/2 lemon
- 3 cloves garlic, minced
- 1 shallot, minced
- 1 tsp dried oregano
- 1 tsp salt
- 1 tsp pepper
- 6 lamb chops

Difficulty:

Prep Time: 1-24 hours

Cook Time: 10-12 min

Serves: 2

Process

1. Combine olive oil, lemon juice, garlic, shallot, oregano, salt, and pepper in a glass jar. Shake vigorously to combine.
2. Rinse chops under cool water, pat dry, and place in a 1-gallon ziplock bag.
3. Pour marinade over chops, seal the bag, and toss to ensure they are evenly coated in the seasoning.
4. Marinate in the refrigerator for 1 to 24 hours.
5. Preheat grill to high heat.
6. Grill chops 5-6 minutes per side.

Serve with

- Sautéed spinach (pg 350)
- Roasted rosemary beets (pg 334)

BBLT | bison, bacon, lettuce, and tomato

The familiar flavors of the venerable BLT bring this bison burger to life. This twist on an American classic is best enjoyed outdoors on a warm summer evening paired with our Cajun sweet potato fries.

Ingredients

- 8 strips bacon (2 per burger)
- 1 lb ground bison
- 1 tsp salt
- 1 tsp pepper
- 1 tsp garlic powder
- 1 tsp onion powder
- 2 tsp smoked paprika
- 1 beefsteak tomato, sliced
- Butter lettuce

Difficulty:

Prep Time: 20 min

Cook Time: 8-10 min

Serves: 2

Process

1. Cook bacon until crispy in a skillet on medium heat, flipping as needed.
2. Remove from heat, and place bacon on a plate lined with paper towels to cool.
3. Preheat grill to medium-high heat.
4. In a large mixing bowl, combine ground meat with salt, pepper, garlic powder, onion powder, and smoked paprika.
5. Form ground meat into 4 equal-sized burger patties.
6. Grill burgers 4-5 minutes per side.
7. Remove from grill and set aside.
8. Carefully place tomato slices on the grill.
9. Grill tomato slices 3 minutes per side.
10. Remove tomatoes from grill.
11. Top the burgers with lettuce, tomato, bacon, and serve.

Serve with

- Cajun sweet potato fries (pg 340)

Notes

Tomatoes have a wonderful flavor when grilled, but they get very soft and can be hard to handle. We recommend grilling them on a grill plate or foil if you must, so they do not fall apart when removing them from the grill.

London broil with balsamic marinade

Oftentimes, good salad dressings also make for great marinades. With this steak recipe, we bring big flavor to the grill by letting the meat bathe in our homemade balsamic dressing for a few hours prior to cooking.

Ingredients

- 1/4 cup extra-virgin olive oil
- 1/8 cup balsamic vinegar
- 1/2 cup red onion, finely chopped
- 4 cloves garlic, smashed and roughly chopped
- 1 tbsp spicy brown mustard
- Salt and pepper to taste
- 1 lb London broil

Difficulty:

Prep Time: 24 hrs

Cook Time: 9-11 min

Serves: 4

Process

1. Combine in a mixing bowl the olive oil, balsamic vinegar, red onion, garlic, mustard, salt, and pepper. Whisk together.
2. Place London broil in a ziplock bag or baking dish and cover with the marinade up to 24 hours prior to cooking.
3. Preheat grill to high heat.
4. Grill London broil on high for 4-5 minutes for the first side.
5. Flip, reduce heat to medium-high, and grill for another 5-6 minutes.
6. Remove from heat, allow to rest 5 minutes, then slice thinly and serve.

Notes

London broil tends to be a tougher cut of meat, being that it is so lean. We recommend allowing the meat to marinate for up to 24 hours to help tenderize the steak before cooking.

Mint "lamburgers"

Juicy "lamburgers" hot off the grill will have your mouth watering before they even hit your plate. The aroma of mint and garlic filling your nose as you grill will have you anxiously awaiting that first bite. Plating these burgers over a deconstructed Greek salad will complete the full effect of this meal.

Ingredients

- 1 lb ground lamb
- 3 cloves garlic, minced
- 1 shallot, minced
- 2 tbsp mint, minced
- Salt and pepper to taste

Difficulty:

Prep Time: 15 min

Cook Time: 8 min

Serves: 4

Process

1. Heat grill to medium heat.
2. Mix ground lamb with minced garlic, shallot, mint, salt, and pepper.
3. Form into 4 equal-sized patties.
4. Grill lamburgers for approximately 4 minutes per side, turning once. Adjust cook time for desired internal temperature accordingly.
5. Garnish lamburgers with a mint leaf.

Serve with

- Greek salad (pg 256)
- Greek salad dressing (pg 304)

Notes

An optional cooking method for the lamburgers is to bake them on a parchment-lined baking sheet at 350 degrees for 25 minutes.

Pulled pork barbecue

One of the great treats of summer is pulled pork barbecue. We make this recipe paleo with a delicious and light barbecue sauce that brings tangy sweet flavors to the pulled pork, without any added sugars.

Ingredients

- 3 lb "Boston butt" pork shoulder
- 1 fist of garlic, peeled
- 3 cups chicken broth
- Barbecue sauce (pg 306)

Difficulty:

Prep Time: 20 min

Cook Time: 8 hrs

Serves: 6-8

Process

1. Rinse pork under cold water and pat dry with a paper towel.
2. Cut slits into the entire pork shoulder and stud with cloves of garlic.
3. Place pork in crock pot and cover with chicken broth.
4. Cook pork on low for 8 hours.
5. While the pork is cooking, make the barbecue sauce.
6. After 8 hours of cooking, remove the pork from crock pot, and let cool.
7. Discard thick layers of fat, connective tissues, or veins.
8. Shred pork by pulling apart the meat using two forks.
9. Toss pork with barbecue sauce, garnish with avocado slices, and enjoy!

Garlic and jalapeño bison burger

If you like your burger with a little kick, then this one is for you. Wrap it up in some big, fresh lettuce leaves and you'll have a cookout hero in your hands.

Ingredients

- 1 lb ground bison
- 2 jalapeño peppers, seeded and minced
- 5 cloves garlic, minced
- 1 tsp salt
- 1 tsp pepper
- Organic sun dried tomatoes for garnish.

Difficulty:

Prep Time: 12 min

Cook Time: 8-10 min

Serves: 2

Process

1. Preheat the grill to medium-high heat.
2. In a large mixing bowl, combine ground bison, jalapeños, garlic, salt, and pepper.
3. Form ground meat and spices into 4 equal-sized patties.
4. Place burger patties on grill and cook 4-5 minutes per side.
5. Remove from grill, top with sun-dried tomatoes and serve.

Notes

If you want your burgers to be spicier, roast the peppers prior to mincing. We would recommend roasting them under the broiler (high heat, about 500°F), bringing the oven rack to the top level, and broiling the peppers for 5 minutes.

Smoky lime rib steaks

The aromas of smoked paprika, cumin, and garlic pair beautifully with the deep, warm flavor of red palm oil. The addition of fresh lime juice adds a crisp, light dimension to this recipe. This marinade is fantastic over any cut of steak, and also makes for a delicious dipping sauce!

Ingredients

- 3 cloves of garlic, chopped
- 1 shallot, chopped
- Juice of 1 lime
- 1 tbsp smoked paprika
- 1 tbsp cumin
- 1/2 tbsp sea salt
- 1/2 tbsp ground pepper
- 1/2 cup red palm oil
- 2 rib steaks

Difficulty:

Prep Time: 1-4 hrs

Cook Time: 15-18 min

Serves: 2

Process

1. Pulse garlic, shallot, lime, and spices in food processor.
2. Slowly add in red palm oil while blending.
3. Blend until mixture is smooth.
4. Pour over steaks and let marinate in refrigerator for 1-4 hours.
5. Preheat oven to broil, with the rack about 6 inches from the flame.
6. Place steaks on a broiling pan and pour remaining sauce over steaks.
7. Broil for about 8 minutes per side for 3/4-inch-thick steaks.

Notes

An alternative way to serve this dish is to use the smoky lime marinade as a dipping sauce. For this we would recommend broiling or grilling the steaks with a light sprinkling of salt on either side, and serving with the marinade for dipping. This marinade would also be fantastic over chicken, fish, or shrimp.

Stuffed banana peppers

These peppers may look harmless, but do not be fooled—they pack quite a punch of spice. Using the recommended tablespoon of seeds will really give you a kick in the pants. You've been warned!

Ingredients

- 8 hot banana peppers, tops and seeds removed. Reserve 1 tbsp of seeds for seasoning
- 1 lb grass-fed ground beef
- 3 cloves garlic, minced
- 1/2 Vidalia onion, finely chopped
- Salt and pepper to taste

Difficulty:

Prep Time: 10 min

Cook Time: 20 min

Serves: 4

Process

1. Rinse banana peppers, and removed ends to seed them.
2. Save 1 tablespoon of the hot pepper seeds to season the ground beef.
3. On medium heat, brown the ground beef, adding the garlic, onion, salt, pepper, and hot banana pepper seeds.
4. Once the meat is cooked, allow to cool.
5. Preheat grill to medium-high heat.
6. Carefully stuff the hot peppers with the ground beef.
7. Grill peppers 8-10 minutes, turning every 2-3 minutes.

Notes

When working with hot peppers, it is always recommended to wear rubber gloves. The seeds can in fact burn your fingers. Make sure to wash your hands after eating them as well, especially before touching your face or eyes. We learned the hard way!

Stuffed bison filets

Bison filets are so tender and juicy they will literally melt in your mouth. The mushrooms and onions, sautéed in a splash of balsamic vinegar, nicely enhance the steaks without overpowering the natural flavors.

Ingredients

- 1 tbsp coconut oil
- 3 cloves garlic, minced
- 1 small yellow onion, thinly sliced
- 1.5 cups shiitake mushrooms, stems removed
- 2 tsp balsamic vinegar
- Salt and pepper to taste
- 2 grass-fed bison tenderloin filets

Difficulty:

Prep Time: 15 min

Cook Time: 20 min

Serves: 2

Process

1. In a frying pan, melt coconut oil on medium heat.
2. Add garlic, onion, and mushrooms to the frying pan and sauté until the onions are translucent and the mushrooms have softened.
3. Pour balsamic vinegar over mushrooms, sprinkle with salt and pepper, and continue to sauté for 3-5 minutes.
4. Remove mushrooms from heat and set aside.
5. Preheat grill to medium heat.
6. Rinse bison filets under cold water and pat dry with a paper towel.
7. Cut a small pocket in each filet, leaving about 1/2 inch between the pocket and the outside of the filet.
8. Stuff the filets with the sautéed mushrooms and onion, leaving remaining mushrooms for garnish.
9. Grill bison filets for 5-7 minutes per side.
10. Top with sautéed mushrooms, and serve.

Notes

Bison is extremely lean, which will yield a faster cook time than conventional beef filet. Keep an eye on these if cooking them for the first time to ensure they do not overcook.

Lamb meatballs with mint pesto

Mint makes a perfect complement for the savory flavors of lamb in any dish. This "pasta" recipe celebrates this classic pairing by emphasizing the flavor of mint in the pesto.

Ingredients

- 1 lb ground lamb
- 1 tsp each of salt, pepper, garlic powder, oregano
- 1 egg, whisked
- 4 medium zucchini
- 1 tbsp extra-virgin olive oil
- 1 clove garlic, minced
- Salt and pepper to taste
- Mint pesto (pg 326)

Difficulty:

Prep Time: 15 min

Cook Time: 30-35 min

Serves: 4

Process

1. Preheat oven to 350°F.
2. Combine ground lamb and spices in a mixing bowl.
3. Add in egg, and stir until evenly distributed.
4. Form mixture into golf-ball-sized pieces.
5. Place on a parchment-lined metal baking sheet.
6. Bake at 350°F for 25 minutes.
7. Cut zucchini into "noodles" with a mandoline.
8. Sauté zucchini in a skillet with 1 tablespoon olive oil, garlic, salt, and pepper. Sauté until zucchini is soft and noodle-like.
9. Toss noodles with mint pesto, then top with lamb meatballs and serve.

Notes

Be aware when cooking the zucchini "noodles" that they will become soft and slightly mushy if overcooked. For a more "al dente" bite, lightly sauté the zucchini for 2-4 minutes until they have just slightly softened.

Cinnamon steak skewers

These skewers bring unique flavors to classic grilled steak. Cinnamon is a great pairing with beef, albeit underutilized. The addition of curry and ginger give this dish a warm and slightly tangy flavor.

Ingredients

- Four, 6 oz steaks
- Juice of 1 lemon
- 1 tbsp extra-virgin olive oil
- 1 tbsp cinnamon
- 1 tsp curry powder
- 1/2 tsp ground ginger
- Salt and pepper to taste

Difficulty:

Prep Time: 1-24 hrs

Cook Time: 12-16 min

Serves: 2-4

Process

1. Soak wooden steak skewers in water for an hour prior to grilling.
2. Cut steaks into cubes and place in a 1-gallon ziplock bag.
3. In a small mixing bowl, whisk together marinade ingredients.
4. Pour marinade over steak, seal ziplock bag, and marinate in the refrigerator at least 1 hour, up to 24 hours.
5. Preheat grill to high heat.
6. Skewer steak onto wooden skewers.
7. Grill skewers 12-16 minutes, turning every 3-4 minutes.
8. Plate steak skewers over your choice of salad and serve.

Serve with

- Asparagus and arugula salad (pg 282)

Notes

This cinnamon rub is fantastic on any cut of steak, and would also be wonderful on bison, as well as chicken.

Prosciutto and arugula pizza

During my years at Penn State, I had the opportunity to spend a semester living in Rome to study urban design. What ensued were four months of sipping cappuccino, teaching myself how to paint and draw, and a lot of incredible pizza. Italian pizza is light, with a thin crust and topped with fresh ingredients. This pizza is our grain-free version of the pizza I so often enjoyed in Italy.

—Bill

Ingredients

- 1 whole eggplant, grated
- 1/4 cup flax seed meal
- 1/4 cup almond meal/flour
- 1 egg
- Salt and pepper to taste
- 1 tsp extra-virgin olive oil
- 1 large Roma tomato, thinly sliced
- 1/4 lb prosciutto
- 1/2 cup arugula
- 1 tsp dried oregano
- 1 tsp dried basil

Difficulty: / / /

Prep Time: 15 min

Cook Time: 60 min

Serves: 4

Process

1. Preheat oven to 350°F.
2. Grate eggplant with a cheese grater, discarding the skin.
3. Place grated eggplant in a clean dish towel, and squeeze over a sink to remove excess liquid.
4. Pour grated eggplant into a large mixing bowl.
5. Add in the flax meal and almond meal.
6. Whisk egg in a smaller bowl and add to batter.
7. Add salt and pepper to taste.
8. Mix until ingredients are evenly combined.
9. Pour batter onto a parchment-lined baking sheet.
10. Smooth batter out with hands into a thin layer about 1/8 inch thick.
11. Bake crust for 30-35 minutes.
12. Remove the crust from oven. Lightly grease another piece of parchment paper with olive oil, and place on top of crust. Carefully flip the crust and then slowly peel off the parchment paper from the bottom side.
13. Brush the flipped side lightly with olive oil.
14. Bake opposite side for about 15 minutes.
15. Remove from oven and apply toppings and spices.
16. Bake for an additional 7-10 minutes, then serve.

Notes

The pizza will be finished once the tomatoes have cooked down and the prosciutto has 'wilted'.

Flank steak with citrus marinade

Located near the belly of the cow, flank steak is juicy and flavorful, though not known for its tenderness. The citrus marinade pairs perfectly with the flank cut because the acid lends itself well to tenderizing the meat and imparting a sweet flavor. Serve it thinly sliced over simply grilled vegetables for an easy, great-tasting meal.

Ingredients

- Juice of 1 blood orange
- Juice of 3 limes
- 4 cloves of garlic, peeled and crushed
- 1 tbsp brown mustard
- 1 tbsp raspberry blush vinegar
- 2-lb flank steak (or skirt steak)
- 1 green onion, sliced to garnish

Difficulty:

Prep Time: 1 hr

Cook Time: 12-14 min

Serves: 4

Process

1. Combine the fresh orange and lime juice and crushed garlic in a small mixing bowl.
2. Add brown mustard and raspberry vinegar to the mixing bowl and whisk all ingredients together.
3. Allow steak to marinate for up to 1 hour in a large ziplock bag in the refrigerator.
4. Remove steak from refrigerator 20-30 minutes prior to grilling.
5. Preheat grill to medium-high heat.
6. Grill flank steak for 6-7 minutes per side on medium heat, turning once.
7. Serve thinly sliced over grilled asparagus or a bed of spring greens.

Serve with

- Grilled asparagus (pg 336)

Lemon thyme lamb chops

Lemon and thyme are often used to compliment the flavor of lamb. For this recipe we used the ever fragrant lemon thyme herb to infuse the olive oil for marinating. This seasoning combines the wonderful flavors of lemon and thyme by use of one simple herb.

Ingredients

- 2 tbsp lemon thyme, chopped
- 1/2 cup extra-virgin olive oil
- 6 lamb chops
- Salt and pepper to taste

Difficulty:

Prep Time: 1-24 hours

Cook Time: 10-12 min

Serves: 2

Process

1. In a small mixing bowl, combine lemon thyme with olive oil.
2. Rinse chops under cool water, and pat dry with a paper towel.
3. Place chops in a large ziplock bag, and pour marinade over the chops.
4. Make sure that each chop is evenly coated in marinade, and allow to marinate in the refrigerator for up to 24 hours.
5. Preheat grill to high heat.
6. Sprinkle lamb chops with salt and pepper.
7. Grill lamb chops for 5-6 minutes per side.
8. Serve with a sprig of fresh thyme.

Serve with

- Greek salad (pg 256)

Notes

If you cannot find lemon thyme, you can easily create the flavors of this dish by using regular thyme and the juice of 1/2 a lemon.

Steak fajitas

Packing quite the spicy kick, this recipe utilizes all the traditional seasonings of fajitas with cumin, chipotle, lime juice, and garlic. This recipe is so delicious you won't even notice the absence of a tortilla!

Ingredients

- 1 lb skirt steak
- 1 tbsp extra-virgin olive oil
- 1 red bell pepper, thinly sliced
- 1 yellow bell pepper, thinly sliced
- 1 Vidalia onion, thinly sliced
- 2 cups baby bella mushrooms, sliced
- 1 tsp each of salt, pepper, chipotle pepper, and cumin

Marinade

- 2 tbsp extra-virgin olive oil
- Juice of 1.5 limes
- 1 tsp each of salt, black pepper, chipotle pepper, and cumin
- 4 cloves garlic, minced

Difficulty:

Prep Time: 24 hrs

Cook Time: 25 min

Serves: 4

Process

1. Rinse skirt steak under cool water and pat dry.
2. Carefully remove any remaining silver skin from the steak.
3. Place steak in a 1-gallon ziplock bag and set aside.
4. In a small mixing bowl, whisk together olive oil, lime juice, salt, pepper, chipotle, cumin, and garlic.
5. Pour marinade over steak, seal bag, and toss to evenly coat the entire skirt steak.
6. Place in the refrigerator and marinate up to 24 hours.
7. Preheat grill to 500°F, 10 minutes prior to cooking.
8. Remove steak from the refrigerator and bring up to room temperature.
9. Grill steak 3-4 minutes per side. Allow to rest for 5 minutes after cooking, then cut steak in thin strips.
10. Heat olive oil on medium heat in a cast-iron skillet.
11. Add vegetables and seasonings, and sauté until onions are translucent and peppers have softened. Remove from heat and set aside.
12. Turn oven to broil at 500°F, and raise oven rack to the top level.
13. Place vegetables in cast-iron skillet under the broiler for 3-5 minutes.
14. Serve steak topped with vegetables, and with a side of guacamole.

Serve with

- Game day guacamole (pg 88)

Braised lamb shanks

Braising is a wise choice of preparation for lamb shanks, as this cut is typically tough. The "low and slow" cooking process results in tender, juicy meat that just falls off the bone.

Ingredients

- 2 tbsp coconut oil
- 2 medium-sized lamb shanks
- Salt and pepper to taste
- 1 onion, chopped
- 1 fist of garlic, cloves unpeeled
- 3 sprigs rosemary
- 5 sprigs thyme
- 3 sprigs oregano
- 1 cup beef broth

Difficulty:

Prep Time: 20 min

Cook Time: 3-4 hrs

Serves: 2

Process

1. Heat 1 tablespoon of the coconut oil in a cast-iron skillet over medium heat.
2. Sear lamb shanks, one at a time, until evenly browned while seasoning with salt and pepper to taste. After first shank is complete, add the remaining tbsp of coconut oil.
3. Place lamb shanks in a crock pot (slow cooker).
4. Sauté the onion and unpeeled garlic cloves in the skillet for 1-2 minutes, seasoning with salt and pepper.
5. Cover the lamb shanks with the sautéed garlic and onion. Place the rosemary, thyme sprigs, and oregano in a securely tied piece of cheese cloth ("bouquet garni").
6. Place bouquet garni in the crock pot, cover all with 1 cup of beef broth.
7. Slow cook for 3-4 hours on low heat.
8. Serve with onions and garlic on top.

Serve with

- Mashed turnips and parsnips (pg 332)

[Poultry]

Rosemary roasted turkey

A holiday feast wouldn't be complete without a golden roasted turkey. Rosemary is our first choice when enhancing the flavor of poultry, and it fills the home with a wonderful aroma during cooking. This recipe is one to enjoy with your entire family or loved ones for any holiday.

Ingredients

- 2 tbsp extra-virgin olive oil
- 6-7 lb turkey breast
- 2 tbsp rosemary, roughly chopped
- Salt and pepper to taste

Difficulty:

Prep Time: 15 min

Cook Time: 2-3 hrs

Serves: 6-10

Process

1. Preheat oven to 325°F.
2. Drizzle olive oil over turkey breast, brush to coat.
3. Separate rosemary from stems, roughly chop and sprinkle liberally on turkey.
4. Add salt and cracked pepper to taste.
5. Place turkey in shallow roasting pan.
6. Cook turkey approximately 25 minutes per pound (turkey is done when a meat thermometer inserted into the breast reads 170°F). Periodically baste turkey with juices in the pan, especially toward the end of the cooking.
7. Let rest for 10 minutes, carve, and serve.

Notes:

To complete this meal, serve alongside carrot soufflé (pg 342), cranberry sauce (pg 340), and strawberry salad (pg 280).

Lemon garlic roasting chicken

The smell of chicken roasting in the oven brings along a feeling of comfort in our home during cold winter months. This recipe, full of flavor, will also fill your home with the wonderful scent of garlic and rosemary during the cooking process.

Ingredients

- 1 roasting chicken
- 1 tbsp minced garlic
- 1 tbsp minced fresh rosemary
- 1 tsp ground pepper
- 1 tbsp lemon zest
- 1.5 tbsp extra-virgin olive oil
- 1/2 lemon

Difficulty:

Prep Time: 20 min

Cook Time: 20-30 min/lb

Serves: 2-4

Process

1. Thoroughly clean chicken, including the body cavity, and remove the giblets and neck. Pat dry with paper towels. Place in a baking dish or roasting pan, breast side up.
2. Preheat oven to roast at 350°F.
3. In a small bowl, combine garlic, rosemary, pepper, lemon zest, and olive oil.
4. Rub herb and oil mixture onto the entire chicken, including inside the body cavity.
5. Cut the leftover lemon in half, and place inside the body cavity of the bird.
6. Roast chicken 20-30 minutes per pound, until it has reached 170°F in the breast, and the juices run clear.
7. Allow to rest for 5 minutes after removing from oven. Carve and serve.

Notes

When garlic burns, it becomes very bitter. To avoid bitter-tasting garlic, omit the minced garlic from the rub, and place whole cloves (the more the merrier!) into the body cavity along with the fresh lemon. This will infuse the chicken with the aroma of garlic and lemon.

Herbed chicken skewers

Perfect for parties, these skewers are a great make-ahead food that people can easily eat while standing. The herb seasoning is nicely balanced, giving the chicken light and fresh flavors.

Ingredients

- 5 lbs chicken tenders
- 1/4 cup extra-virgin olive oil
- 1/4 cup herbs de Provence
- Zest of 1 lemon
- Salt and pepper to taste

Difficulty:

Prep Time: 30 min

Cook Time: 15 min

Serves: 10

Process

1. Rinse chicken tenders under cold water and pat dry with a paper towel.
2. Carefully remove the tendon with a knife.
3. Cut tenders into large chunks.
4. In a large mixing bowl, combine chicken, olive oil, herbs de Provence, lemon zest, salt, and pepper.
5. Cover bowl with plastic wrap, and marinate for 2-4 hours.
6. Preheat grill to medium-high heat.
7. Skewer chicken and grill for 12-15 minutes, turning every 3-4 minutes until meat is completely opaque.

Notes

If using bamboo skewers, be sure to soak them in water for at least one hour prior to grilling so they do not burn or catch on fire.

Stuffed turkey breast

We firmly believe that turkey should be enjoyed year-round, and not just on holidays. This preparation is still cause for celebration, but can be enjoyed any night of the week without extra fanfare.

Ingredients

- 4-lb boneless, skin-on turkey breast
- 2 cups white mushrooms, chopped
- 2 cups baby spinach, chopped and stems removed
- 1 cup white onion, chopped
- 3 cloves garlic, minced
- 2 tbsp fresh rosemary, minced
- Salt and pepper to taste
- 2 tbsp extra-virgin olive oil

Difficulty:

Prep Time: 25 min

Cook Time: 25 min/lb

Serves: 6-8

Process

1. Preheat oven to roast at 375°F.
2. In a non stick skillet, sauté mushrooms, baby spinach, onion, garlic, and rosemary in 1 tablespoon olive oil until mushrooms have softened slightly. Season with salt and pepper. Remove from heat and set aside.
3. Carefully remove skin from turkey and set aside.
4. Place turkey breast, skin side down on a large cutting board.
5. Spread halves of breast apart, so the turkey breast opens like a book.
6. Release thickest tenders of meat with a sharp knife so that you can open the breast more to create an even thickness of meat.
7. Cover turkey breast with parchment paper and carefully pound to even thickness with a meat mallet (or cast-iron skillet like we had to resort to using). You want the meat to be as even as possible without damaging the breast.
8. Spread stuffing over turkey and tightly roll the breast for roasting.
9. Cover the stuffed breast with the reserved skin, and tie with kitchen twine in three evenly spaced intervals to keep skin in place.
10. Lay stuffed breast in a roasting pan or baking dish, seam side down.
11. Lightly rub skin with olive oil.
12. Roast at 375°F for about 2 hours and 30 minutes, or until the roast has reached 175°F in the breast.

Notes

It helps to have an extra pair of hands to help with this dish. We recommend having a pair of hands to roll the turkey, and a helper to tie it up for cooking. The finished product is well worth the work!

Baked chicken thighs

The dark meat of the chicken is full of wonderful flavor, and becomes even more delicious when allowed to cook in its own juices from the fatty skin. For this recipe, we place shallot and garlic under the skin to infuse the chicken with flavor, and simply sprinkle salt and pepper over top. The crisp skin adds the perfect crunch when taking that first juicy bite!

Ingredients

- 4 free-range bone-in, skin-on chicken thighs
- 1 shallot, minced
- 3 cloves garlic, minced
- Salt and pepper to taste

Difficulty:

Prep Time: 10 min

Cook Time: 40-45 min

Serves: 2

Process

1. Preheat oven to bake at 425°F.
2. Rinse chicken thighs under cold water and place in a broiler pan.
3. Pat thighs dry with a paper towel.
4. Gently separate skin from thigh, without removing it completely from the corners.
5. Place shallots and garlic under the skin.
6. Sprinkle the skin with salt and pepper.
7. Bake for 40-45 minutes, or until juices run clear.

Notes

To complete this dish, serve with a fresh salad, or your choice of lightly cooked vegetables.

Chicken with 40 cloves of garlic

This is a popular dish that has been shared by many respectable cooks. Often, this recipe calls for the use of liquor and white wine. For our version, we keep things simple and allow the flavors of the chicken to be enhanced only by bathing in herbs (and a massive amount of garlic) for a few hours. Do not get so caught up in the tender and juicy chicken that you forget to enjoy the steamed cloves of garlic. They are a wonderful little treat in their own right.

Ingredients

- 1 roasting chicken
- 3 tbsp coconut oil
- 3-4 fists of garlic, cloves separated, unpeeled
- 1 handful rosemary
- 1 handful lemon thyme
- 1 shallot, minced
- Salt and pepper to taste

Difficulty: 🥢🥢

Prep Time: 20 min

Cook Time: 1.5 hrs

Serves: 4-6

Process

1. Cut chicken into eight pieces (2 wings, 2 drumsticks, 2 thighs, 2 breasts).
2. Heat a skillet to medium heat with 1 tablespoon coconut oil.
3. Sear chicken on all sides, set aside in a large mixing bowl.
4. Sauté garlic in coconut oil until the skin of the garlic begins to soften and brown slightly.
5. Place half of the garlic on the bottom of a Dutch oven.
6. Place the chicken on top of the garlic.
7. Cover with the remainder of the garlic, pour in the juices from the bowl, and top with rosemary, thyme, shallot, salt, and pepper.
8. Cover with a lid, and roast at 350°F for 1.5 hours.

Notes

Keeping the skin on the cloves of garlic allows them to steam while cooking. This results in the garlic infusing the chicken with flavor, while cooking for a long time without burning.

Turkey meatloaf

Meatloaf was a staple in my house growing up, which we enjoyed on a regular basis. I can remember eating slice after slice, always wanting just a bit more. Perhaps the only reason I would spare some of the loaf would be to leave some for the next day to be enjoyed as leftovers. This meatloaf brings back fond memories of "Mom's meatloaf" . . . good luck leaving any to be enjoyed the next day, though!

— Bill

Ingredients

- 2 lbs lean ground turkey
- 1 egg, whisked
- 2 tbsp coconut aminos
- 1 tsp garlic powder
- 1 tsp salt
- 1 tsp pepper
- 1/2 cup chopped onion
- 1/2 cup green pepper, chopped
- 1/2 cup celery, chopped

Difficulty:

Prep Time: 15 min

Cook Time: 60 min

Serves: 6-8

Process

1. Preheat oven to bake at 375°F.
2. Combine all ingredients in a large mixing bowl.
3. Lightly grease a loaf pan with coconut oil.
4. Pour ground turkey mixture into the loaf pan. Evenly distribute the mixture to get a uniform loaf.
5. Bake at 375°F for one hour.
6. Remove from oven and let rest for 10 minutes.
7. Slice, and serve!

Notes

This recipe will work best with a perforated loaf pan with drip holes on the bottom (and a matching catch pan for the drippings).

Duck confit

Bring a bit of French cooking into your kitchen without much fuss. Traditional duck confit takes several days to make. In our version the work is scaled back to a few hours, while preserving all the wonderful flavors.

Ingredients

- 2-4 duck legs, skin on, bone in
- Salt
- 10 cloves garlic, unpeeled
- 10 sprigs thyme
- 1 tsp coconut oil

Difficulty:

Prep Time: 70 min

Cook Time: 2 hrs

Serves: 2-4

Process

1. Rinse duck legs under cold water, and pat dry with a paper towel.
2. Using a sharply pointed knife, poke small holes into the skin at an angle. These holes will allow the fat to seep out from under the skin, and make the skin crispy during cooking. Do not pierce the meat.
3. Place duck legs in a large mixing bowl. Sprinkle generously with salt and coat both sides.
4. Cover bowl with plastic wrap, and allow to sit at room temperature up to 1 hour.
5. Place garlic cloves and thyme in an even layer in a baking dish just large enough to fit the duck legs.
6. Place duck legs on top of garlic and thyme, skin side up.
7. Rub the duck skin with coconut oil.
8. Place the duck in the oven and heat oven to bake at 285°F.
9. Bake for 2 hours.

Serve with

- Haricots verts (pg 350)

Notes

Pricking the skin of the duck allows for the fat to release during cooking. Classic duck confit is duck leg cooked in duck fat. You can also add extra duck fat, if you have it on hand, to cook the duck in as well.

Cumin-spiced chicken

Ground cumin brings a warm, earthy flavor to these chicken skewers, which nicely compliments the sweet flavor of the bell peppers. The addition of an aioli sauce made from red palm oil really brings this dish together.

Ingredients

- 4 (4- to 6-oz) chicken breasts
- 2 tbsp extra-virgin olive oil
- 1 tbsp ground cumin
- 1/2 tbsp garlic powder
- 1/2 tbsp onion powder
- 1 tsp black pepper
- 1 red bell pepper, chopped
- 1 yellow bell pepper, chopped
- 1 orange bell pepper, chopped

Difficulty:

Prep Time: 1 hr

Cook Time: 12-15 min

Serves: 4

Process

1. Rinse chicken under cold water and pat dry with a paper towel.
2. Cut chicken into 1-inch cubes, and place in a large ziplock bag.
3. Drizzle olive oil over chicken, and sprinkle with spices.
4. Combine spices with chicken using a spoon or your hands to insure all chicken is evenly coated with the spices.
5. Seal bag, and place in the refrigerator to marinate for at least an hour.
6. Preheat grill to medium-high heat.
7. Remove chicken from fridge and skewer chicken and bell peppers, alternating chicken with peppers.
8. Grill skewers 12-15 minutes, rotating every 4 minutes.

Serve with

- Red palm aioli (pg 328)

Notes

To evenly coat chicken with spices, you can seal the bag and massage the chicken through the bag. Then open the bag, and mix by hand to make sure everything is coated. The chicken skewers will be ready to turn when the chicken easily releases from the grill.

Smoked paprika chicken thighs

The strong smoky aroma of smoked paprika brings bold flavors to these succulent chicken thighs. The sweet, warm undertones of the smoked paprika and cumin will have your mouth watering before that first juicy bite into the crispy skin of the thighs.

Ingredients

- 4 bone-in, skin-on, organic chicken thighs
- 1 tsp smoked paprika
- 1 tsp garlic powder
- 1 tsp ground cumin
- 1/4 tsp cayenne pepper
- 1 tbsp red palm oil
- Salt and pepper to taste

Difficulty:

Prep Time: 10 min

Cook Time: 40-45 min

Serves: 2

Process

1. Preheat oven to bake at 425°F.
2. Rinse chicken thighs, pat try with a paper towel, and place in a large ziplock bag.
3. In a small mixing bowl, combine smoked paprika, garlic powder, cumin, cayenne, and red palm oil.
4. Pour seasoning over chicken, seal bag, and toss until the chicken is fully coated.
5. Place chicken thighs on a broiling pan, and sprinkle with salt and pepper.
6. Bake at 425°F for 40-45 minutes.

Notes

We love serving chicken thighs at parties in place of wings. These are a great option for a dinner on your own, but sure are a crowd pleaser. Try them out for your next house party!

Balsamic and rosemary chicken

The warm, sweet aroma of fresh rosemary is enhanced in this dish by the sweet flavor of balsamic vinegar. This recipe is one of our favorite ways to enjoy chicken breasts. Served alongside a bed of fresh greens, this entrée is always one to please.

Ingredients

- 3 boneless, skinless chicken breasts
- 1 tbsp extra-virgin olive oil
- Salt and pepper to taste
- 2 cloves garlic, minced
- 2 tsp fresh rosemary, minced
- 1/4 cup balsamic vinegar

Difficulty:

Prep Time: 15 min

Cook Time: 20-25 min

Serves: 3

Process

1. Rinse chicken breasts under cold water, pat dry with a paper towel, and place in a baking dish.
2. Drizzle olive oil over all 3 chicken breasts, and lightly rub to evenly distribute the oil.
3. Sprinkle salt and pepper over chicken.
4. Press fresh garlic and rosemary into chicken breasts.
5. Roast at 400°F for about 20-25 minutes or until the meat yields an internal temperature of 170°F.
6. Remove chicken from oven and pour 1/4 cup balsamic vinegar over fully cooked chicken breasts.
7. Serve with a fresh sprig of rosemary.

Notes

An alternate cooking method would be to grill the breasts. You can also easily recreate this dish using split breasts that are bone in and skin on.

Spaghetti squash with turkey tomato sauce

This is the first recipe that I concocted on my own after making the transition to a paleo lifestyle. This recipe was also the first time I tried using coconut oil. The sauce is delicious and great on its own, and the flavors only get better the following day.

— Hayley

Ingredients

- 1 tbsp coconut oil
- 1 Vidalia onion, chopped
- 1 medium-to-large zucchini, chopped
- 1 lb lean ground turkey
- 1 tsp cayenne pepper
- 1 tsp garlic powder
- 1 tsp onion powder
- 2 cans of tomato sauce, plus 1/2 can of water
- 1 pack sliced white mushrooms
- Baked spaghetti squash (pg 348)

Difficulty:

Prep Time: 10 min

Cook Time: 30 min

Serves: 4-6

Process

1. In a medium frying pan, heat 1 tablespoon of coconut oil.
2. Add onion and zucchini to the frying pan and sauté in coconut oil until both onion and zucchini are tender. Remove from heat.
3. Brown the ground turkey in a large soup pot on medium heat.
4. Once the turkey is fully cooked, add the sautéed onion and zucchini, and season with cayenne pepper, garlic powder, and onion powder.
5. Pour two cans of tomato sauce, and half a can of water over the ground turkey and veggies.
6. Add in sliced mushrooms.
7. Bring sauce to a boil, then turn down to a simmer and cover.
8. Simmer for 20-30 minutes, or until the mushrooms are tender.

Notes

We use Muir Glen tomato sauce for this recipe, because it has no added salt and all natural ingredients. It's always best to go salt free and add the salt in yourself if desired.

Chicken satay

Although typically served with a peanut sauce, our version of this Thai dish is complimented with a tangy sunbutter-based dipping sauce. This tasty recipe is perfect for parties, and sure to be a crowd pleaser.

Ingredients

- 1 cup coconut milk
- 3 cloves garlic, grated
- 1-2 tsp, fresh ginger, grated
- 1 tbsp curry powder
- 1 tsp salt
- 2.5 lbs chicken tenders

Difficulty:

Prep Time: 2-4 hrs

Cook Time: 8-12 min

Serves: 5-6

Process

1. Combine coconut milk, garlic, ginger, curry powder and salt in a small mixing bowl. Mix until evenly combined.
2. Marinate chicken with mixture for 2-4 hours.
3. Soak wooden skewers for a minimum of 1 hour, prior to grilling.
4. Preheat grill to high heat.
5. Skewer chicken tenders with the pre-soaked wooden skewers.
6. Grill over medium-high heat for 8-12 minutes, turning as necessary to cook evenly.
7. Serve with "peanut" satay sauce (pg 318).

Tacos with jicama shells

We love lettuce-wrapped tacos, and taco salads, but with the addition of jicama in place of the typical corn flour shells, you really experience the full effect of a tasty taco recipe. The jicama adds the perfect crunch to this dish!

Ingredients

- 1 large jicama
- 1 lb ground beef or turkey
- 2 cups lettuce, loosely packed
- 1/4 red onion, julienned
- 1 cup guacamole
- Cilantro and lime wedges for garnish

Seasoning

- 2 tbsp chili powder
- 1.5 tbsp cumin
- 1.5 tbsp paprika
- 1 tbsp onion powder
- 1 tbsp garlic powder
- 2 tsp oregano
- 1/2 tsp red pepper flakes

Difficulty:

Prep Time: 30 min

Cook Time: 10-15 min

Serves: 8

Process

1. Peel jicama and slice as thinly as possible using a mandoline or a sharp knife.
2. Soak jicama slices in cold water for 30 minutes prior to serving.
3. Place ground beef or turkey in a skillet and cook on medium heat until no longer pink.
4. Add seasonings and stir until evenly distributed.
5. Pat jicama slices dry, and top with lettuce, meat, game day guacamole (pg 88), onion, and roasted Roma salsa (pg 90).
6. Garnish with cilantro and lime wedges, and serve.

Notes

The jicama slices will be much more flexible after soaking in water for 30 minutes, thus making them more pliable for the tacos.

Chicken and vegetable "lo mein"

Homemade Chinese food was a frequent request for dinner when I was growing up. After going primal, I began to miss some of my favorite Chinese dishes. This recipe brings some familiar Eastern flavors together for a fabulous reinterpretation of chicken and vegetable lo mein.

—Bill

Ingredients

- Toasted sesame oil
- 1 tbsp minced ginger
- 1 tbsp minced garlic
- 1 lb chicken, cubed
- 2 cups broccoli
- 1/2 cup water chestnuts
- 1/4 cup celery, chopped
- 1/2 cup shiitake mushrooms, stems removed and cut in half
- 1/4 cup almonds, chopped
- 2 cups shredded cabbage
- 1/4 cup green onion, chopped
- 1/4 cup coconut aminos
- Sesame seeds to garnish

Process

1. Heat wok or skillet over high heat.
2. Add sesame oil, minced ginger and garlic, and sauté for 1 minute to allow the flavors to infuse the oil.
3. Add chicken to the wok, and cook, stirring frequently for 3-4 minutes, or until the chicken is mostly cooked.
4. Add in broccoli, water chestnuts, celery, and shiitake mushrooms; sauté for 2 minutes.
5. Add in almonds, cabbage, and green onion.
6. Pour in coconut aminos (2-4 tbsp).
7. Cook 2-3 minutes, until cabbage softens a little.
8. Remove from heat, and garnish with sesame seeds.

Difficulty:

Prep Time: 20 min

Cook Time: 15 min

Serves: 4-6

Notes

Alternative protein options for this dish would be beef, bison, pork, or shrimp. All would be delicious!

Grilled turkey drumsticks

If you've never tried grilling turkey drumsticks, you're missing out! These big, juicy cuts are perfect for grilling. Keep the flame low, and these babies will come out perfectly tender with a nice crisp skin.

Ingredients

- 1 tbsp cumin
- 1 tbsp garlic powder
- 1/2 tsp cayenne
- 1/2 tsp sea salt
- 1 tsp pepper
- 2 turkey legs (drumsticks)
- 3 tbsp red palm oil

Difficulty:

Prep Time: 8 min

Cook Time: 60-70 min

Serves: 2

Process

1. Preheat grill to medium-high heat.
2. Mix together cumin, garlic powder, cayenne, sea salt and pepper in a small bowl.
3. Rub drumsticks with seasonings.
4. Sear drumsticks on the grill for approximately 3 minutes per quarter turn.
5. After searing all sides, move drumsticks to a part of the grill where they can cook by indirect heat. (See notes below).
6. Cook drumsticks via indirect heat for an additional 50-60 minutes. The grill temperature during this time should read around 300°F. Turn drumsticks 1/4 turn every 10 minutes until they have reached an internal temperature of 180°F.
7. Baste drumsticks with red palm oil toward the end of their cook time, about the last 20 minutes or so. Reapply as necessary.

Notes

This recipe uses an indirect cooking technique on the grill. If you have a gas grill, turn one burner off and leave the remaining burners lit at medium heat. Place the drumsticks over the burner that has been shut off. If you have a charcoal grill, move the drumsticks to the coolest spot on the grill or raise the rack. The objective is to slowly cook the turkey so that it does not burn or dry out.

Spaghetti and meatballs

Bookmark this page, because when your friends hear that pasta is "out" with paleo, you can quickly turn to it and say "not so fast!" This dish will definitely give you your spaghetti fix, along with some amazing meatballs.

Meatballs

- 1 lb ground turkey, or choice of ground meat
- 3/4 cup onion, finely chopped
- 1 egg, whisked
- 2 tbsp coconut aminos
- 1 tsp each of garlic powder, salt, and pepper

Marinara

- 3/4 cup chopped onion
- 2 tbsp minced garlic
- 1 tbsp extra-virgin olive oil
- 2 cans diced tomatoes, no salt added
- Salt and pepper to taste
- 1 tsp oregano
- 2 tbsp fresh flat-leaf parsley, finely chopped

Spaghetti

- spaghetti squash

Difficulty: / / /

Prep Time: 15 min

Cook Time: 35-45 min

Serves: 4

Process

1. Preheat oven to bake at 350°F.
2. In a medium-sized mixing bowl, combine ground meat, onion, egg, coconut aminos, garlic powder, salt, and pepper.
3. Form ground meat mixture into 1-inch balls, and place on two parchment-lined baking sheets.
4. Bake at 350°F for 25 minutes.
5. In a sauce pan, sauté onion and garlic in olive oil on medium heat.
6. Once onion and garlic have reduced and infused the olive oil with flavor, add two cans of diced tomatoes.
7. Add salt, pepper, oregano, and parsley to sauce and stir, combining all ingredients.
8. Bring sauce to a boil, turn down to simmer, and let simmer for 20 minutes covered. If sauce starts to boil when covered, then remove lid.
9. While sauce is simmering, cut spaghetti squash in half and remove seeds.
10. Microwave each half for 10 minutes, and scoop out squash with a fork into a bowl. Alternative cooking method is baking the spaghetti squash (pg 348).
11. Toss spaghetti squash "noodles" with sauce, top with meatballs, and serve.

Grilled split chicken breasts

Lemon and garlic are classic flavors often paired with chicken. For this dish, the lemon and garlic, along with the shallot, infuse the chicken under the skin, resulting in wonderful flavor, all tucked under crispy grilled skin.

Ingredients

- 2 split chicken breasts, bone in and skin on
- 3 cloves of garlic, minced
- 1 lemon, thinly sliced
- 1 shallot, thinly sliced
- Salt and pepper to taste

Difficulty:

Prep Time: 10 min

Cook Time: 15-25 min

Serves: 2

Process

1. Preheat grill to high heat.
2. Rinse chicken under cold water and set aside. Pat dry with a paper towel.
3. Carefully lift the skin from the breast creating a space to stuff.
4. Place the garlic, lemon, and shallot under the skin, and stretch the skin a bit to cover the stuffing.
5. Sprinkle the chicken with salt and pepper
6. Place chicken breasts on grill, bone side down and cook for 10-15 minutes, depending on the thickness of the breasts.
7. Carefully flip the chicken, grill for 5-7 minutes on breast side.
8. If the chicken needs to cook longer than this time, flip it back to the bone side, reduce heat to medium-high, and cook until meat is white (or 165°F in the thickest part of the breast).

Serve with

- Roasted broccoli (pg 338)

Notes

You can create this recipe using bone-in chicken thighs as well. Another option would be to roast a whole chicken and stuff it with fresh lemon, garlic, and shallot.

Red curry chicken skewers

We love any excuse to use coconut milk in a recipe, and coconut milk plays a large role in this tasty Thai dish. With a simple red curry seasoning, these skewers are a great way to bring the flavor of Thai cuisine to your table.

Ingredients

- 1/4 cup coconut milk
- 1 tbsp red curry paste
- 1/4 tsp salt
- 4 boneless, skinless chicken breasts
- 1 Vidalia onion, chopped
- 2 green bell peppers, seeded and chopped

Difficulty: / / /

Prep Time: 70 min

Cook Time: 20 min

Serves: 4

Process

1. Whisk the coconut milk, curry paste, and salt together in a small bowl for the curry sauce.
2. Cut chicken into chunks.
3. Place chicken in a ziplock bag, and pour curry sauce over chicken to marinate.
4. Marinate chicken in the refrigerator for up to an hour.
5. Cut onion and green pepper into chunks.
6. Preheat grill on medium-high heat.
7. Skewer the meat and vegetables using metal (or wood) skewers. If you use wood, soak the skewers for an hour prior to grilling.
8. Cook skewers, turning 1/4 turn every 5 minutes until evenly cooked.
9. Let rest for 5 minutes before serving.

Serve with

- Cauliflower rice (pg 348)

Notes

To add the curry flavor to the vegetables as well, you can marinate them, along with the chicken in the same bag.

Portobello turkey burgers

One of our very first recipes we posted on our blog was for portobello turkey burgers. The use of a big juicy portobello mushroom cap is a tasty replacement for the typical grain-filled bun. Serve this alongside sweet potato fries for a classic summertime meal.

Ingredients

- 1 large tomato, sliced
- 1 onion, sliced thickly
- 1 lb ground turkey or ground beef
- 4 large portobello mushroom caps, gills removed
- Lettuce for garnish

Seasoning

- 1 tsp garlic powder
- 1 tsp onion powder
- 1 tsp salt
- 1 tsp pepper

Difficulty:

Prep Time: 15 min

Cook Time: 15 min

Serves: 3-4

Process

1. Preheat grill to high heat.
2. Rinse and slice vegetables (slice tomato to 1/8 inch thick and onion to about 1/4 inch).
3. Place turkey in a medium-sized mixing bowl and combine with seasoning ingredients. Mix until the spices are evenly distributed.
4. Form turkey into four equal-sized patties.
5. Grill turkey burgers on high for approximately 5 minutes per side, flipping once.
6. Grill the onion and portobello caps on high for 3-4 minutes.
7. Serve the burger atop the portobello cap with lettuce, onion, and tomato.

Serve with

- Cajun sweet potato fries (pg 340)

Notes

Portobello mushrooms release a lot of liquid when cooked, to avoid a soggy "bun", remove the gills underneath the cap prior to grilling.

Pineapple-glazed chicken skewers

The use of fresh pineapple to glaze grilled chicken will bring a sweet tropical flavor to your plate. These are a perfect party dish for a summer luau!

Ingredients

- 1 cup pineapple, diced
- 1/4 cup extra-virgin olive oil
- 3 cloves garlic, minced
- 1 tbsp ginger, minced
- Juice of 1 lemon
- 1 tsp salt
- 1 tbsp cilantro, minced
- 3 chicken breasts
- 3 cups pineapple, cut into chunks

Difficulty:

Prep Time: 20 min

Cook Time: 12-15 min

Serves: 3

Process

1. Combine diced pineapple, olive oil, garlic, ginger, lemon juice, and salt in a small bowl.
2. Puree mixture in a blender or food processor.
3. Pour back into the small mixing bowl, and stir in the minced cilantro, set aside to use as glaze during grilling
4. Preheat grill to medium-high heat.
5. Skewer pieces of chicken and pineapple on metal or pre-soaked bamboo skewers.
6. Grill skewers for 12-15 minutes, turning every 4-5 minutes. Brush the chicken with the pineapple glaze periodically while grilling.
7. Garnish skewers with chopped cilantro, and serve.

Serve with

- Roasted broccoli (pg 338)
- Grilled fennel (pg 354)

Notes

The natural sugar that releases from pineapple when cooked, may cause a sticky situation for the grill grates. The chicken and pineapple tends to have trouble releasing, so we recommend lightly oiling a grill plate to use, or grilling the skewers on top of foil.

[Seafood]

Crab cakes

For a few years after college, I lived in Washington, D.C., which happens to be a fantastic place for enjoying blue crabs. During my time there, I had the pleasure of eating many, many crab cakes. These crab cakes bring a taste of Maryland to your dinner plate.

—Bill

Ingredients

- 16 oz wild-caught lump blue crab meat.
- 1 egg, whisked
- 2 tbsp mayonnaise (pg 312)
- 1 shallot, minced
- 1 tbsp flat-leaf parsley, chopped
- 1 tbsp Old Bay seasoning
- Seafood mustard sauce (pg 310)

Difficulty:

Prep Time: 15 min

Cook Time: 25 min

Serves: 4

Process

1. Preheat the oven to bake at 350°F.
2. In a large mixing bowl, combine crab meat, egg, mayo, shallot, parsley, and Old Bay seasoning.
3. Form crab mixture into cakes, about the size of the palm of your hand.
4. Place cakes on a parchment-lined baking sheet.
5. Sprinkle tops of cakes with additional Old Bay seasoning.
6. Bake for 25 minutes.
7. Top crab cakes with the mustard sauce and serve.
8. Garnish with parsley, fresh chives, or a lemon wedge.

Crab-stuffed salmon

This dish is inspired by a creation of my sister Nellie and her husband, Chris. According to Nellie," as long as we've been together, whenever Chris wanted to make a nice meal for me, it was always crab-stuffed salmon. To this day, it is still a go-to recipe if we want to treat ourselves."

—Bill

Ingredients

- 16 oz wild-caught lump blue crab meat
- 3 cloves garlic, minced
- 3 tbsp fresh parsley, minced
- Juice of 1/2 lemon
- A dash of salt and pepper
- 4 center-cut wild salmon filets

Difficulty:

Prep Time: 10 min

Cook Time: 25 min

Serves: 4

Process

1. Preheat oven to bake at 400°F.
2. In a small bowl, season crab meat with minced garlic, parsley, the juice of half of a lemon and salt and pepper.
3. Slice salmon filet lengthwise down the center to create a space for stuffing.
4. Stuff salmon with seasoned crab meat, using about 1/4 cup of crab per salmon filet.
5. On a broiling pan, bake salmon for 18 minutes at 400°F.
6. Switch to broil, move rack to the top position, and broil salmon at 500°F for an additional 5 minutes.
7. Garnish with fresh parsley and lemon.

Notes

This recipe will make about 1-1.5 cups of extra crab mixture. We typically bake the extra crab in soufflé dishes and save it for a leftover treat the next day.

Grilled mahi mahi with mango chutney

This dish should perhaps read "mango chutney with grilled mahi mahi," as the chutney really is the star of the show. This spicy, warm, sweet sauce just dances on your tongue and brings the mahi mahi to life. This condiment of Southeast Asian origin pairs well with most white fish, and chicken as well.

Ingredients

- Juice of 1 lemon
- 1/2 cup extra-virgin olive oil
- 1 tsp salt
- 1 tsp black pepper
- 1 tsp red pepper flakes
- 3 cloves garlic, chopped
- 4 mahi mahi filets, 5-6 oz each
- Mango chutney (pg 310)

Difficulty:

Prep Time: 30 min

Cook Time: 20 min

Serves: 4

Process

1. Combine marinade ingredients in a food processor until well blended.
2. Marinate the fish in a ziplock bag for up to 1 hour before grilling.
3. Heat grill to medium heat (about 400°F). If you have a fish plate for your grill, allow it to preheat as well.
4. Place fish on the grill, skin side down first.
5. Cook for 4-5 minutes before flipping.
6. Cook opposite side for 4-5 minutes, until fish is opaque in the center.
7. Serve topped with mango chutney and a sprig of cilantro.

Notes

To complete this dish, serve with a side of cauliflower rice (pg 348), or steamed vegetables.

Jamaican jerk salmon

Classic Jamaican jerk spices bring new and exciting flavors to this salmon dish. Jamaican jerk seasoning often uses brown sugar to add sweet flavor to offset the spicy kick that it gives. To make this paleo, we omitted the sugar and just let the spices enhance this meal on their own.

Ingredients

- 1 lb wild-caught salmon, cut into 4-6 oz portions
- 1 tsp all spice
- 1 tsp cinnamon
- 1 tsp ginger
- 1 tsp cumin
- 1 tsp smoked paprika
- 1 tsp garlic powder
- 1 tsp onion powder
- 1/4 tsp thyme
- 1/4 tsp cayenne pepper
- 1 tsp salt
- 2 tbsp extra-virgin olive oil
- Juice of 1.5 limes

Difficulty: / / /

Prep Time: 2-4 hours

Cook Time: 8 min

Serves: 2

Process

1. Rinse salmon under water and pat dry with a paper towel.
2. Cut salmon into 4-6 oz portions, and place in a 1-gallon ziplock bag.
3. In a small mixing bowl, whisk together spices, olive oil, and lime juice.
4. Pour marinade over salmon, seal bag, and make sure the salmon is evenly coated in the marinade.
5. Marinate salmon for 2-4 hours prior to grilling.
6. Preheat grill to 400°F.
7. Place salmon on a fish plate, skin side down first, and grill for 4 minutes a side, flipping once.
8. Serve over a bed of greens.

Notes

This Jamaican jerk seasoning would be fantastic over chicken and shrimp as well as the salmon.

Cedar plank salmon with lime

Nothing quite says "summer" like the smoky aroma of cedar on the grill. These simple yet delicious salmon filets are an easy way to win over dinner guests. Present the salmon right on the cedar plank to finish this dish with panache.

Ingredients

- 4 wild-caught salmon filets
- 1 tbsp coconut oil, melted
- Black pepper to taste
- Juice of 1 lime

Difficulty:

Prep Time: 1-2 hrs

Cook Time: 10-15 min

Serves: 4

Process

1. Soak cedar planks for 1-2 hours prior to cooking.
2. Preheat grill to high heat.
3. Lightly brush salmon filets with melted coconut oil.
4. Sprinkle with black pepper.
5. Place wet cedar planks on the grill. Lay salmon filets on the cedar planks. Reduce heat to medium-high.
6. Cook salmon on planks, without flipping, for 10-15 minutes or until cooked through.
7. Squeeze lime juice over salmon and serve on the cedar planks.

Serve with

- Cauliflower rice (pg 348)

Notes

Keep a glass of water on hand to prevent the planks from catching on fire, if necessary. Cedar planks bring great flavor to any cut of fish. To complete this dish serve with a fresh salad or cauliflower rice.

Pan-seared scallops

The use of coconut oil in this recipe enhances the naturally sweet flavor of fresh scallops. This recipe is one that is perfect as an entrée, and would also be a fantastic appetizer for guests.

Ingredients

- 12 scallops
- 1 tbsp coconut oil
- 2 shallots, minced
- Salt and pepper to taste

Difficulty:

Prep Time: 8 min

Cook Time: 4 min

Serves: 2-4

Process

1. Rinse scallops with cold water and pat dry with a paper towel, set aside.
2. Heat coconut oil in a frying pan.
3. Add minced shallots to coconut oil and sauté until shallots are translucent.
4. Add scallops to frying pan, and sprinkle with salt and pepper.
5. Sear scallops for approximately 2 minutes per side.

Notes

Be cautious when cooking scallops. They tend to cook quickly, and can become tough or chewy when overcooked. They will be fully cooked when opaque throughout.

Grilled curry shrimp

This recipe is a great way to bring some exotic flavors to simple grilled shrimp. We play up the warm aroma of red palm oil by seasoning the shrimp with curry, garlic, coriander, and ginger. The warm, sweet flavors of this dish are out of this world. Plate the shrimp over a bed of cauliflower rice for the perfect finishing touch.

Ingredients

- 1 lb raw, peeled, tail on shrimp
- 1/8 cup red palm oil
- 2 tsp curry powder
- 1 tsp ground coriander
- 1 tsp garlic powder
- 1/2 tsp ground ginger
- Salt and black pepper to taste

Difficulty:

Prep Time: 1 hr

Cook Time: 8 min

Serves: 4

Process

1. Rinse shrimp under cold water and pat dry with a paper towel.
2. Place shrimp in a large ziploc bag.
3. In a small mixing bowl, combine red palm oil, curry powder, coriander, garlic powder, ground ginger, salt, and pepper.
4. Pour spice mixture over shrimp, seal bag, and toss to evenly coat.
5. Place shrimp in the refrigerator and allow to marinate for at least an hour.
6. Preheat grill to high heat.
7. Grill shrimp on a fish plate, or in a grill basket (grill wok), stirring occasionally, until the shrimp are opaque (about 8 minutes).

Serve with

- Cauliflower rice (pg 348)

Halibut en papillote

"En papillote" means to cook in paper. For this recipe we steam fish, vegetables, and herbs in parchment paper to create a complete dish. This results in a meal full of flavor, lightly cooked, in a quick amount of time.

Ingredients

- 2 (4- to 6-oz) halibut filets
- Cracked black pepper to taste
- 1 shallot, thinly sliced
- 1/2 lemon, thinly sliced
- 1 small bunch garlic scapes

Difficulty:

Prep Time: 10 min

Cook Time: 15 min

Serves: 2

Process

1. Preheat oven to bake at 400°F.
2. Rinse halibut under cold water, and pat dry with a paper towel.
3. Place individual pieces of halibut on their own large sheet of parchment paper (approximately 15" x 15").
4. Sprinkle halibut with black pepper.
5. Top with shallot, lemon, and garlic scapes (about 2 scapes per cut of fish).
6. Moving from one end to the other, roll the parchment paper inward toward the halibut, creating a sealed "pouch" for the fish.
7. Place on baking sheet, and bake for 15 minutes (this is for a 1-inch-thick cut of fish—adjust the time according to thickness).

Notes

Open the parchment with caution, as there will be hot steam inside. Feel free to create this recipe using any cut of fish you like, and additional vegetables if desired. You can also use different cuts of meat for en papillote as well (adjust cook time accordingly).

"Linguine" with clams

One of my favorite meals growing up was when my mom would make linguine in clam sauce. We make this old-time favorite of mine paleo by using spaghetti squash, seasoned only from the sautéed vegetables, and topped with clams fresh off the grill.

—Hayley

Ingredients

- 1.5 tbsp extra-virgin olive oil
- 3 cloves garlic, minced
- 1/2 shallot, minced
- 1 cup baby asparagus tips
- 3 cups shiitake mushrooms, stems removed, cut in half
- Salt and pepper to taste
- 20 small clams, grilled
- Baked spaghetti squash (pg 348)

Difficulty: / / /
Prep Time: 15 min
Cook Time: 30 min
Serves: 4

Process

1. Preheat grill to high heat.
2. In a frying pan, heat 1 tablespoon of olive oil over medium heat.
3. Sauté garlic and shallot in olive oil until translucent.
4. Add asparagus and continue to sauté for one minute.
5. Add mushrooms, drizzle with 1/2 tablespoon olive oil. Sprinkle with salt and pepper, and continue to sauté for 5-7 minutes or until mushrooms are soft.
6. Remove mushrooms and asparagus from heat.
7. Add baked spaghetti squash to the frying pan and toss with the mushrooms and asparagus.
8. Place clams on a hot grill, and cook until the clams pop open. Remove clams from the grill once they open.
9. Place the squash, mushrooms, and asparagus mixture in a bowl. Top with clams, and serve.

Notes

Clams that are open prior to cooking should not be consumed. On the other hand, any clams that do not open during cooking should not be consumed either.

Simply grilled salmon

The simple marinade for this salmon is our go-to marinade for chicken, fish, or shrimp. It is also fantastic over lamb, and would pair well with pork as well. The lemon in this marinade brings fresh flavor to the deep aromas of the basil and oregano.

Ingredients

- 1 lb wild-caught salmon
- 1/4 cup extra-virgin olive oil
- Juice of 1 lemon
- 2 cloves garlic, minced
- 1 tsp dried basil
- 1 tsp dried oregano
- 1 tsp salt
- 1 tsp pepper

Difficulty:

Prep Time: 1 hrs

Cook Time: 8-10 min

Serves: 3-4

Process

1. Rinse salmon under cold water, pat dry with a paper towel, and cut into 4 equal-sized portions.
2. In a glass jar, combine olive oil, fresh lemon juice, garlic, basil, oregano, salt, and pepper. Seal jar and shake vigorously to combine.
3. Place salmon in a 1-gallon ziplock bag, pour marinade over salmon, seal and toss to ensure the salmon is fully coated in the marinade.
4. Marinate in the refrigerator for up to 1 hour prior to grilling.
5. Preheat the grill to medium-high heat.
6. Grill salmon 4 minutes per side over medium-high heat.

Serve with

- Cucumber and tomato salad (pg 266)

Shrimp scampi

Shrimp scampi is often served over rice or pasta in a buttery garlic sauce. For our version, we butterfly the shrimp, tossing them in garlic, olive oil, and parsley and baking them. To experience the complete scampi experience, plate your shrimp over baked spaghetti squash or cauliflower rice.

Ingredients

- 3 large cloves garlic, minced
- 1 tbsp fresh parsley, chopped
- 1 lb raw, peeled, tail-on shrimp
- 3 tbsp extra-virgin olive oil
- Salt and pepper to taste

Difficulty:

Prep Time: 1 hr

Cook Time: 15 min

Serves: 4

Process

1. Rinse shrimp under cold water and remove tails if desired.
2. Mince garlic and parsley and set aside.
3. Using a paring knife, slice shrimp along the back side from head to tail. Do not cut through the shrimp.
4. Place shrimp in a large ziplock bag.
5. Pour olive oil over shrimp and cover with garlic, parsley, salt, and pepper.
6. Close ziplock bag and let marinate for up to 1 hour.
7. Preheat oven to bake at 350°F.
8. Open shrimp to lay flat on a parchment-lined baking sheet.
9. Bake at 350°F for 15 minutes.

Notes

When butterflying shrimp, only cut halfway through the shrimp. You want the shrimp to easily open, without being split in half.

Steamed Maryland crabs

Back when I used to live in Washington, D.C., my friends and I would often go to the Maine Street Wharf and get a bushel of steamed Maryland crabs. Evenings spent enjoying blue crabs are quite memorable. This dish takes me back to those warm summer evenings spent with great friends in D.C.

—Bill

Ingredients

- 2 cups water
- 1.5 cups apple cider vinegar
- 1/4 cup Old Bay seasoning
- 1/2 tbsp salt
- 12 large, live blue crabs

Difficulty:

Prep Time: 10 min

Cook Time: 20-30 min

Serves: 4

Process

1. In a large bowl, combine water, vinegar, and seasonings.
2. Place a steamer basket in a large pot.
3. Place 6 live crabs on top of the steamer basket.
4. Pour approximately half of the seasoning mixture from the bowl over the crabs.
5. Add the remaining crabs, and top with the remaining seasoning mixture.
6. Cover with a tightly fitting lid and place a heavy object on the lid to prevent any crabs from escaping.
7. Steam crabs for 20-30 minutes, until crabs are bright red.

Serve with

- Grilled asparagus (pg 336)
- Garlic butter (pg 320)

Notes

When ordering crabs, it is typically best to get the largest ones your fish monger has. These are typically referred to as " Number Ones" or " Number One Jimmies."

Sushi

Our first date as a couple was to a great little sushi place in Pittsburgh. We'll always have fond memories of that date, though when we want to revisit the flavors we make this great rice-free version instead.

Ingredients

- 1 head of cauliflower
- 1/2 tbsp coconut oil
- 1 cucumber
- 1 avocado
- 6 squares nori seaweed
- 1/2 cup wild-caught lump blue crab meat

Difficulty:

Prep Time: 20 min

Cook Time: 5-7 min

Serves: 3-4

Process

1. Rinse cauliflower, and grate with a cheese grater. Discard stems.
2. Sauté cauliflower in 1/2 tablespoon of coconut or olive oil for 5-7 minutes on medium heat. Let cool.
3. Thinly slice cucumber and avocado.
4. Place a sheet of seaweed onto a cutting board, and cover 2/3 with a thin layer of cauliflower.
5. Place a row of cucumber, avocado, and crab meat 1/2 inch from the top edge of the seaweed.
6. Carefully roll sushi until you have an inch of seaweed left. Wet the sea weed with water to seal the roll.
7. Slice sushi roll into 1-inch pieces.
8. Serve sushi with wasabi and coconut aminos for dipping.

Serve with

- Wasabi and coconut aminos as condiments.

Notes

You can also enjoy this recipe using sushi-grade tuna, salmon, or even cooked shrimp.

Seared ahi tuna with wasabi mayo

Being sushi lovers, a seared tuna recipe was a must for this book. The wasabi mayonnaise truly brings out the best in the ahi, providing a savory touch with a hint of heat.

Ingredients

- 1 tbsp sesame oil
- 2 tbsp coconut aminos
- 1 tsp red pepper flakes
- 1/4 tsp fish sauce
- 3 cloves garlic, minced
- 1 tbsp ginger, minced
- Juice of 1/2 lime
- 2 ahi tuna steaks
- 1 tsp pure wasabi power
- 1/4 cup mayonnaise (pg 312)

Difficulty:

Prep Time: 2-4 hrs

Cook Time: 6-7 min

Serves: 2

Process

1. Combine first seven ingredients in a small mixing bowl and whisk together.
2. Place tuna steaks in a ziplock bag with marinade, and allow to marinate for 2-4 hours prior to cooking.
3. Preheat grill to high heat.
4. Place tuna steaks on preheated grill and sear on each side (approximately 3 minutes per side for rare tuna).
5. Add 1 tsp pure wasabi powder to 1/4 cup of mayonnaise (pg 312), and stir to evenly mix.

Notes

Consuming undercooked fish increases your risk of food-borne illness, be sure to always purchase fresh, sushi-grade tuna when serving rare.

Salads and Soups

Soup and salad are perfect additions to any main course and, when paired together, can make a delicious entrée on their own. In this section we have created several simple salads that bring wonderful fresh flavors to the table, as well as salads that would make a fantastic main course on their own. We have also created some delicious soups for any season. Have fun mixing and matching the recipes in this section with your favorite entrée or simply serve them on their own. Either way, they will shine.

Fennel and orange salad

This salad is all about fun texture counterpoints. The juicy, sweet pop of the orange plays off of the crisp, thinly sliced red onion and crunchy slivered almonds. Thinly sliced fennel finishes the dish nicely by contributing a unique flavor to this great little salad.

Ingredients

- 1 fennel bulb
- 1 radish
- 1/4 cup red onion
- 2 oranges
- Orange vinaigrette (pg 304)
- 1/4 cup almonds, slivered

Difficulty:

Prep Time: 10 min

Cook Time: 5 min

Serves: 2

Process

1. Slice fennel, radish, and onion using a mandoline (or slice thinly using a sharp knife).
2. Cut orange into bite-sized chunks, discarding the outer skin and inner membranes.
3. Toss fennel, onion, radish, and orange with orange vinaigrette.
4. Top with a sprig of fennel greens and some slivered almonds.

Asian steak salad

When it comes to steak, I usually just want a good grilled sirloin with just a pinch of salt on it. Not so with this tasty steak salad. The marinade for the steak imparts incredible flavor, so to me, the salad is simply a bonus on top of an amazing steak dish.

—Bill

Steak Marinade

- 2 tbsp coconut aminos
- 2 tbsp fish sauce
- 1/2 tsp each, salt and pepper
- Red pepper flakes, to taste
- 1 clove garlic, minced
- 1/2 tbsp ginger, minced

Ingredients

- 10 oz sirloin steak
- 1.5 cups shredded cabbage
- 1/4 red bell pepper, sliced thin
- 1 radish, sliced thin
- 1 medium carrot, shredded
- 8 grape tomatoes, halved
- 1/2 navel orange, chopped
- 1/8 cup slivered almonds
- 1/2 green onion, chopped
- Sesame ginger dressing (pg 322)

Difficulty:

Prep Time: 3 hrs

Cook Time: 10 min

Serves: 2

Process

1. Whisk together marinade ingredients and pour over steak. Allow steak to marinate 3 hours before cooking.
2. Preheat grill to high heat.
3. Grill sirloin steak on high heat for approximately 4 minutes per side, flipping once.
4. While letting the steak rest, rinse and chop all vegetables, as well as the orange.
5. Toss cabbage, bell pepper, radish, tomato and orange in a medium-sized mixing bowl.
6. Slice the steak thinly (1/8-inch strips).
7. Plate salad, and top with strips of the sirloin. Add slivered almonds and green onion as garnish.
8. Drizzle with sesame ginger dressing and serve.

Pear and walnut salad

Soft juicy pears, tart dried cherries, and crunchy raw walnuts create a fantastic sweet and savory salad tossed with simple greens. Dressed with our white balsamic vinaigrette, each bite will have the flavors dancing on your tongue.

Ingredients

- 1/2 cup dried cherries
- 3/4 cup raw walnuts
- 2 Bosc pears, very ripe
- 5 cups, mixed spring greens

Difficulty:

Prep Time: 10 min

Serves: 4

Process

1. Cut pears into chunks, chop walnuts, and slice cherries in half.
2. Toss with spring greens.

Serve with

- Raspberry vinaigrette (pg 308)

Greek salad

This salad is our go-to side dish for any time lamb is on our menu. Our simple Greek salad is perfect plated under "lamburgers," paired with grilled lamb chops, or even with roast leg of lamb.

Ingredients

- 5 cups spring mix greens
- 3 Roma tomatoes, halved
- 1 green bell pepper, thinly sliced
- 1/2 medium red onion, thinly sliced
- 1 cup sliced cucumber
- 1/4 cup capers
- 1/2 cup black or kalamata olives

Difficulty:

Prep Time: 15 min

Serves: 3-4

Process

1. Toss spring greens with Roma tomatoes, green bell pepper, red onion, and sliced cucumber.
2. Top salad with capers and olives.

Serve with

- Greek salad dressing (pg 304)
- Mint "lamburgers" (pg 148)

Colorful cauliflower salad

This fresh salad adds gorgeous color to your plate. The flavors of all the vegetables in this salad are so wonderful on their own that all you need to dress this salad is a touch of olive oil and fresh lime.

Ingredients

- 1/2 head cauliflower
- 1/2 red bell pepper
- 1/2 yellow bell pepper
- 1 cup carrot
- 1 cup cucumber
- 1 cup cherry tomatoes
- 3 radishes
- 2 green onions
- 2 tbsp parsley
- 1 tbsp extra-virgin olive oil
- Juice of 1 lime

Difficulty:

Prep Time: 20 min

Serves: 6

Process

1. Grate cauliflower. Place in a bowl, and microwave for 45 seconds on high.
2. Rinse all vegetables, and cut into 1/2-inch chunks.
3. Add chopped vegetables to grated cauliflower.
4. Add in parsley, and stir.
5. Drizzle 1 tablespoon of olive oil, and squeeze the juice of 1 lime over salad.
6. Toss to mix and serve.

Sunflower sprout salad

Sunflower sprouts are a delicious side on their own, but our favorite way to enjoy them is tossed into a green salad. For a touch of color and flavor, we added grated carrots and hearts of palm to complete this salad.

Ingredients

- 1 cup sunflower sprouts
- 2 large carrots, grated
- 2 green onions, chopped
- 2 hearts of palm, chopped
- 2 cups spring mix salad greens
- Juice of 1 lemon
- 1 tbsp extra-virgin olive oil

Difficulty:

Prep Time: 15 min

Serves: 2

Process

1. Rinse spouts under cool water, and allow to dry on a dish cloth.
2. Rinse and peel carrots, and grate using a cheese grater. Set aside.
3. Rinse green onions under cool water, pat dry, and chop into bite-size pieces.
4. Chop hearts of palm into bite-size pieces.
5. Toss all ingredients with greens, drizzle with freshly squeezed lemon and olive oil.

Notes

If your local organic grocer does not have sunflower spouts on their shelves, it is a simple and fun project to grow them yourself. To start sprouting, you'll need one bag of organic potting soil, a small bag of organic sunflower seeds, one paint strainer bag from your hardware store, one medium-sized mixing bowl, filtered water, and a potting tray.

Put around 1 cup of seeds into the mixing bowl, cover with filtered water, place the paint strainer bag over the bowl and soak the seeds overnight in a dark cabinet. The next morning, thoroughly rinse the seeds, leaving the paint strainer bag in place. The strainer bag helps to keep the sunflower seeds contained in the bowl while rinsing them. For the next 3 days, keep the seeds in the dark cabinet and rinse them 3 times throughout the day to keep them moist. After 3 days, plant the seeds in a shallow seed tray with good potting soil, and water 3 times per day for about 5 days. After 5 days, harvest your seeds using scissors, cutting them about 1/2 inch above the soil line.

Grilled chicken salad

A big fresh salad, topped with grilled chicken is a quick, easy, and delicious option for lunch or dinner. We love to throw in as many fresh veggies as we can, top it with simply seasoned chicken, and a drizzle of homemade balsamic dressing.

Ingredients

- 2 chicken breasts, sliced
- 1 celery stalk, chopped
- 1/2 cucumber, chopped
- 1 head broccoli, chopped
- 1 tomato, cubed
- 1/2 red onion, thinly sliced
- 1/2 small jicama, julienned
- 1/3 cup black olives
- 5 cups spring salad greens

Difficulty:

Prep Time: 15 min

Cook Time: 14-20 min

Serves: 4

Process

1. Preheat grill to medium-high heat.
2. Grill chicken breasts for 7-10 minutes per side on medium-high heat, flipping once.
3. Slice chicken into 1/4-inch strips, set aside.
4. Rinse and chop all vegetables.
5. Toss vegetables with spring salad greens.
6. Top with grilled chicken, drizzle with dressing, and serve.

Serve with

- Balsamic vinaigrette (pg 312)

Notes

Feel free to use steak, fish, hard boiled eggs, or your protein of choice to top over this salad. We will often even throw in some seasoned ground meat.

Golden beet salad

Here in our little corner of Pennsylvania, golden beets are only seen in the stores every so often. When we do come across them, this salad instantly gets planned for an upcoming meal. We love the way the warm and tender beets compliment the cool, sweet crunch of the Fuji apples.

Ingredients

- 3 large golden beets, boiled
- 1 medium Fuji apple, chopped
- 5 cups spring mix lettuce
- 1/3 cup slivered almonds
- Avocado oil
- White balsamic vinegar

Difficulty:

Prep Time: 10 min

Cook Time: 45 min

Serves: 4

Process

1. Thoroughly scrub beets clean under cold water.
2. Place beets in a large pot of water, and boil until soft when poked with a fork (about 45 minutes).
3. Remove skin from beets, then chop into bite-sized pieces. Allow to cool before adding to the salad.
4. Rinse and chop the Fuji apple.
5. Toss spring mix greens with the apple and slivered almonds.
6. Add in the cooked beet chunks.
7. Drizzle salad with avocado oil and white balsamic vinegar, and serve.

Notes

The skin of the beets should easily peel off if cooked for the proper amount of time.

Cucumber and tomato salad

This salad would be the perfect antipasto, that is, if pasta were a part of the paleo diet. We regularly make this salad to take on picnics or for casual midweek dinners on the back porch. Despite having sophisticated flavors, this salad easily "dresses down" for any occasion.

Ingredients

- 2 cups cucumber
- 2 cups grape tomatoes
- 1 cup kalamata olives
- 1 tbsp fresh basil, thinly sliced
- 1 tbsp fresh oregano, chopped
- 1 clove garlic, minced
- 2 tbsp extra-virgin olive oil
- 2 tbsp balsamic vinegar
- Cracked black pepper to taste

Difficulty:

Prep Time: 10 min

Serves: 4

Process

1. Rinse and peel cucumber. Slice down the middle, then remove seeds. Chop into bite-sized pieces.
2. Rinse grape tomatoes, slice in half.
3. Thinly slice basil, chop oregano, mince garlic.
4. Toss all ingredients with the kalamata olives in a medium mixing bowl, drizzle with olive oil and balsamic vinegar, and sprinkle with black pepper.

Notes

As an option for this recipe, forgo the olive oil and balsamic vinegar for our balsamic vinaigrette dressing (pg 312).

Prosciutto and arugula salad

Prosciutto is often complimented by the flavors of fruit, and usually a sweeter fruit. For this salad we used fresh grapefruit. It adds a bit of fresh sweet flavor, and also the acidity in the fruit replaces the need for vinegar, so you only need a splash of olive oil to dress the salad.

Ingredients

- 1 medium grapefruit (or 1/4 cantaloupe)
- 1 cup raw walnuts, chopped
- 4 slices of prosciutto, cut into strips
- 4 cups arugula, loosely packed
- Drizzle of extra-virgin olive oil
- Salt and cracked pepper to taste

Difficulty:

Prep Time: 15 min

Serves: 2

Process

1. Peel skin from grapefruit. If you're feeling fancy, remove the outer membrane from the wedges. Cut into bite-sized pieces.
2. Chop 1 cup of raw walnuts, set aside.
3. Cut prosciutto into small ribbons, about 1 inch wide.
4. Plate 2 cups of arugula per plate.
5. Top arugula with prosciutto, grapefruit, and walnuts.
6. Drizzle olive oil over salad. Sprinkle with salt and cracked black pepper if desired.

Hayley's chicken salad

A taste of gourmet is brought to this chicken salad, by the use of flavorful dark meat chicken, roasted and shredded, and all tossed in our rosemary and garlic aioli. All you need is a fresh lettuce leaf to complete this dish.

Ingredients

- 8 chicken thighs, bone in and skin on
- Garlic and rosemary aioli (pg 322)
- Salt and pepper to taste

Difficulty:

Prep Time: 15 min

Cook Time: 45 min

Serves: 4

Process

1. Preheat oven to 425°F.
2. Roast chicken thighs in a baking dish for 45 minutes.
3. Remove from oven and allow to cool.
4. Separate the meat from the skin and bones.
5. Shred the chicken meat with a pair of forks.
6. Toss the shredded meat with the rosemary garlic aioli, adding more bit by bit until the desired creaminess is achieved.
7. Sprinkle with salt and pepper to taste.
8. Serve atop large leaves of Bibb or red leaf lettuce.

Asian broccoli slaw

A simple broccoli slaw is a colorful way to bring flavor and crunch to your plate. The warm flavor of sesame oil is enhanced by the fresh garlic and ginger in this dressing. Broccoli and cabbage has never tasted better than it does in this simple side salad!

Ingredients

- 1/2 small red cabbage, thinly sliced
- 4 cups broccoli, grated
- 2 green onions
- Sesame ginger dressing (pg 322)

Difficulty:

Prep Time: 15 min

Serves: 4

Process

1. Thinly slice 1/2 of a red cabbage using a mandoline or sharp knife.
2. Using a grater or food processor, grate broccoli to uniform small chunks.
3. Chop green onions into 1/4-inch pieces.
4. Toss everything together with the sesame ginger dressing.

Spring slaw with smoked shrimp

The use of fresh vegetables in this colorful slaw adds the perfect crunch to every bite of smoky shrimp. A garnish of crispy bacon brings out the wonderful flavors of smoked paprika in this dish. This meal makes for a fantastic side dish at a party, as well as an entrée for two.

Ingredients

- 1/2 head green cabbage, shredded
- 1/4 cup carrots, shredded
- 2/3 cup celery, chopped
- 2/3 cup red radishes, thinly sliced
- 1/4 cup green onion, chopped
- 1/2 cup flat-leaf parsley, chopped
- 1.5-2 lbs uncooked shrimp
- 3 tbsp extra-virgin olive oil
- 1 tsp smoked paprika
- Salt and pepper to taste
- 1 tbsp minced garlic
- 4 strips bacon, cooked and chopped

Difficulty: / / /
Prep Time: 20 min
Cook Time: 15 min
Serves: 4

Process

1. Rinse and prepare all vegetables, set aside.
2. In a large bowl, toss shrimp, olive oil, paprika, salt, pepper, and minced garlic.
3. Preheat a large nonstick frying pan to medium heat.
4. Sauté shrimp until they turn pink and are opaque. Remove from heat.
5. Cook 4 strips of bacon over medium-low heat until crispy. Remove from heat and allow to cool before chopping.
6. Toss shrimp with slaw until evenly combined.
7. Sprinkle with chopped bacon, and serve.

Artichoke and avocado salad

We love pairing avocado with artichokes and hearts of palm. Simply tossed with fresh greens, and homemade balsamic dressing, this will quickly turn into your favorite quick salad. Top it off with your favorite grilled protein, and you will have a delicious meal complete in no time at all!

Ingredients

- 1 avocado
- 5 cups spring greens
- 1/2 cup artichoke hearts
- 2 hearts of palm

Difficulty:

Prep Time: 10 min

Serves: 4

Process

1. Cut avocado in half, remove pit and skin. Chop into 1/2-inch pieces.
2. Toss spring greens, artichoke hearts and hearts of palm in bowl.
3. Add chopped avocado and gently toss a little more.
4. Drizzle with your choice of dressing.

Serve with

- Balsamic vinaigrette (pg 312)

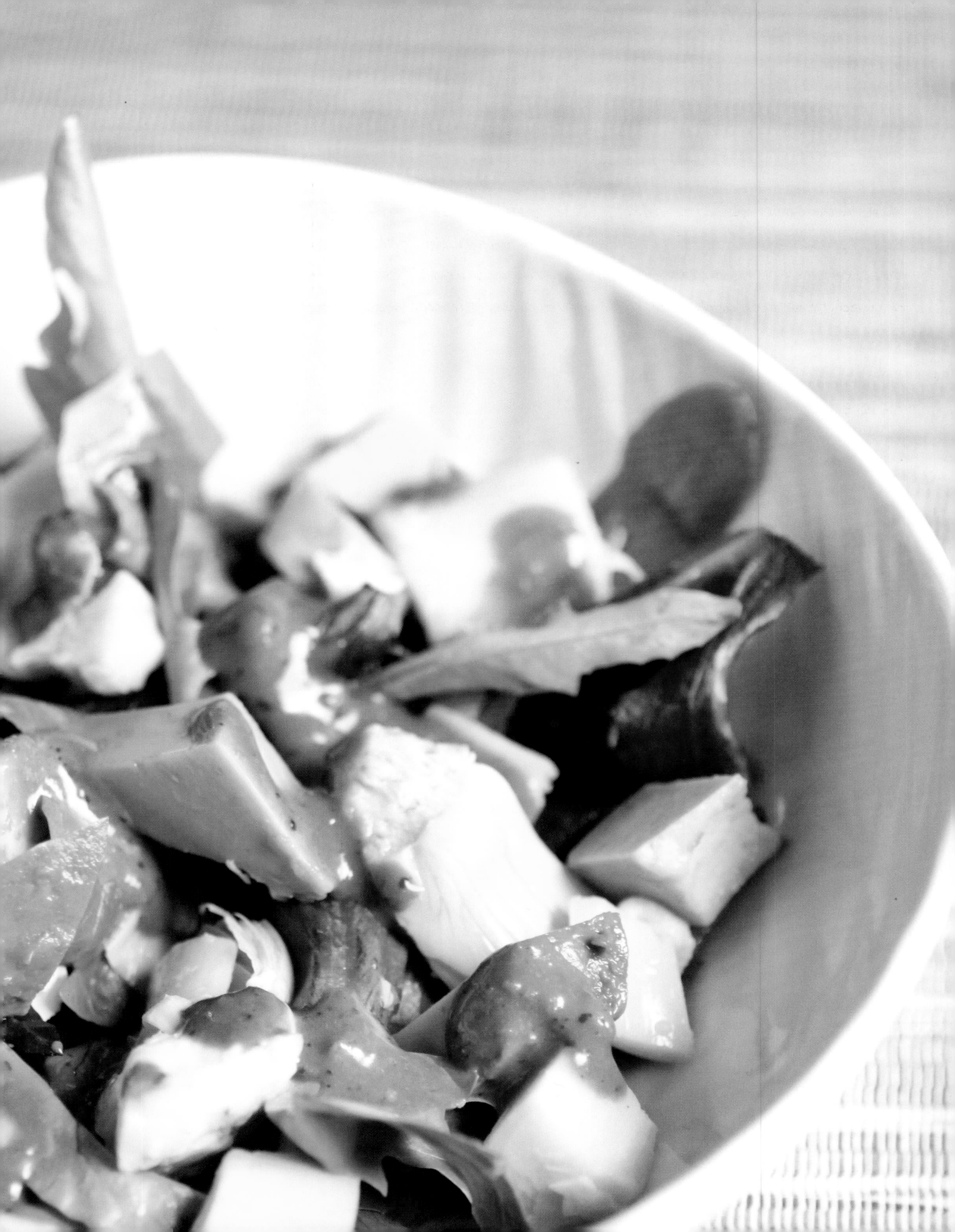

Taco salad

Nothing says you can't still enjoy taco night when you live a grain-free lifestyle! This recipe takes classic taco flavors and deconstructs them to create a deliciously fresh salad. Enjoy this meal for lunch or dinner any day of the week!

Ingredients

- 1 lb ground bison
- 8 cups mixed salad greens
- 1 red bell pepper, julienned
- 1/2 of a red onion, julienned
- 10 cherry tomatoes, sliced in half
- 1 avocado, skin and pit removed and chopped
- 1/2 cup cilantro
- Juice of 1/2 lemon
- Buffalo sauce (pg 324)

Seasoning

- 1 tsp each of: smoked paprika, garlic powder, cumin, chipotle, and black pepper

Difficulty:

Prep Time: 10 min

Cook Time: 10 min

Serves: 4

Process

1. Brown bison in a large skillet over medium heat.
2. Once bison is no longer pink, top with seasonings and stir until meat is evenly coated in spices.
3. Remove seasoned meat from heat and allow to cool slightly.
4. Rinse, dry, and prepare all vegetables.
5. Plate 2 cups lettuce per serving, and top each plate with red bell pepper, red onion, cherry tomatoes, ground bison, avocado, cilantro, freshly squeezed lemon, and a drizzle of buffalo sauce.

Notes

You can also substitute the bison for ground turkey, beef, or pork if you desire. Another great option would be to top this salad with guacamole (pg 88) instead of the chopped avocado.

Strawberry salad

Springtime here in the 'Burgh means two things: sunny days, and fresh local strawberries. This salad is a celebration of our favorite season, bursting with vibrant colors, sweet flavors, and crunchy textures.

Ingredients

- 4 cups spring mix greens
- 6 fresh strawberries, thinly sliced
- 1/4 red onion, thinly sliced
- 1/4 cup walnuts, chopped
- Raspberry vinaigrette (pg 308)

Difficulty:

Prep Time: 8 min

Serves: 2

Process

1. Top spring mix greens with sliced strawberries, sliced red onion, and chopped walnuts.
2. Drizzle lightly with raspberry vinaigrette.
3. Lightly toss, and serve.

Caesar salad

Ingredients

- 2 heads romaine lettuce, chopped
- 2 tbsp Caesar dressing (pg 314)
- Fresh anchovies

Difficulty:

Prep Time: 12 min

Serves: 4

Process

1. Rinse and chop romaine lettuce.
2. Toss with Caesar dressing.
3. Top with a couple fresh anchovies, and serve.

Asparagus and arugula salad

Ingredients

- 2 cups arugula
- 1/2 cup raw asparagus, sliced
- 2 tsp avocado oil
- 2 tsp balsamic vinegar

Difficulty:

Prep Time: 10 min

Serves: 2

Process

1. Toss arugula with asparagus.
2. Drizzle with avocado oil and balsamic vinegar.

Serve with

- Cinnamon steak skewers (pg 162)

Asparagus soup

Light and creamy asparagus soup is a great dish for spring. Perfect for slightly chilly evenings, this soup will bring warmth and fresh flavor to your table.

Ingredients

- 1 Vidalia onion, chopped
- 3 cloves garlic, minced
- 1 tbsp coconut oil
- 2 lbs fresh asparagus, ends removed, and chopped into 1-2 inch pieces
- 1 quart (4 cups) chicken stock
- Salt and pepper to taste

Garnish

- 2 tbsp chopped chives
- 1 cup chopped prosciutto (or pancetta), sautéed
- Ground black pepper

Difficulty:

Prep Time: 15 min

Cook Time: 20 min

Serves: 6

Process

1. In a large soup pot on medium heat, sauté onion and garlic in coconut oil, adding salt and pepper to taste. Sauté until the onion becomes translucent.
2. Add the asparagus to the pot, and cover with the chicken broth.
3. Cover the pot with a lid and boil the asparagus until soft and tender.
4. In a medium-sized frying pan, sauté prosciutto for 5 minutes, set aside.
5. Transfer the soup to a food processor, or high-speed blender, and process until smooth. (You want a smooth, creamy soup. No chunks of asparagus.)
6. Pour into soup bowls and sprinkle with ground pepper, prosciutto, and chives.

Chili

During the long winter months here in Pennsylvania, we crave hearty meals that warm us up after being out in the cold. A piping hot bowl of this chili is the perfect winter evening meal, with tender chunks of beef and spice-infused vegetables. It makes the chilly months a lot more bearable!

Ingredients

- 1 yellow onion, chopped
- 2 green peppers, chopped
- 1 fist garlic, peeled and chopped
- 2 tsp coconut oil
- 3-4 lbs rump roast, cubed
- 1 tbsp smoked paprika
- 2 tsp cumin
- 1 tsp chipotle
- 1 tsp salt
- 1 tsp ground black pepper
- 6 oz tomato paste (small can)
- 30 oz fire-roasted tomatoes, diced (two medium cans)

Difficulty: / / /

Prep Time: 20 min

Cook Time: 3-4 hrs

Serves: 6

Process

1. Rinse and chop the onion and pepper. Peel the garlic and give it a rough chop.

2. Heat a cast-iron skillet over medium heat with 1 teaspoon coconut oil.

3. Sauté the onion and garlic until the onion starts to turn translucent. Transfer to a large soup pot.

4. Sauté the peppers for 3-5 minutes to give a slight char. Add to large soup pot.

5. Add remaining 1 teaspoon of coconut oil to skillet and sear the cubed meat, approximately 5 minutes. Add to large soup pot.

6. Add seasonings and continue to cook over medium heat, stirring the beef through the peppers and the onion. Add the diced tomatoes and tomato paste, continue to stir until the tomato paste dissolves into the chili.

7. Cover, reduce heat to low, and simmer for 3-4 hours.

Notes

When searing the cubed beef, it will release juices naturally. If the skillet is overwhelmed with juices, the steak will not get a good sear. Pour off some of the excess juices so that only 1/2 cup remains in the skillet. Add these juices back into the chili to enhance its flavor.

Pot roast

Part of the enjoyment with this recipe, for me, is the warm, rich aromas that waft through the house as the pot roast cooks. By the time dinner rolls around, there is great anticipation for the meal at hand. The best part about this recipe is that it is simple to make and can provide leftovers for several additional meals.

—Bill

Ingredients

- 4-5 carrots, peeled and sliced
- 1 large onion, cut into chunks
- 5 turnips, quartered
- 2 parsnips, peeled and cut into chunks
- 3 lb chuck roast
- 2 cups beef broth
- 1 tbsp salt and pepper
- Bouquet garni: thyme, sage, 1 bay leaf, and 3-5 cloves garlic

Difficulty:

Prep Time: 25 min

Cook Time: 6-8 hrs

Serves: 6-8

Process

1. Rinse and chop all vegetables.
2. Place vegetables to cover the bottom of a crock pot dish.
3. Place chuck roast on top of vegetables, and place remainder of vegetables around roast.
4. Pour in two cups of beef broth, and sprinkle salt and pepper over the top.
5. Place lid on crock pot, and cook on low for 6-8 hours. About 1-2 hours before finishing, place bouquet garni into the crock pot and continue to cook on low.

Butternut squash soup

The perfect soup to warm your soul on a crisp fall evening, pureed squash brings together all the flavors of autumn to your bowl. Naturally sweet butternut squash is enhanced beautifully by the use of cinnamon in this recipe. Chopped walnuts give this meal just the right amount of crunch. This soup will have all your senses soaring.

Ingredients

- 1 onion, chopped
- 2 tbsp coconut oil
- 1 tsp cinnamon
- 1/2 tsp nutmeg
- 1 tsp salt
- 1 medium butternut squash, peeled and chopped
- 1 quart chicken stock

Difficulty:

Prep Time: 15 min

Cook Time: 30-40 min

Serves: 6-8

Process

1. Sauté chopped onion in coconut oil in a large pot.
2. Add in cinnamon, nutmeg, and salt.
3. Add chopped butternut squash to pot, and pour in broth.
4. Boil the butternut squash in the broth until tender.
5. Puree soup in a food processor or high-speed blender until smooth.
6. Garnish with a sprinkling of cinnamon and chopped walnuts.

Tropical fruit gazpacho

This sweet, tropical fruit soup is refreshing on a hot summer day. A fun treat to serve at a summer cookout, this fresh soup also makes for a tasty dessert!

Ingredients

- 1 pineapple, chopped
- 1 mango, chopped
- 1/2 cucumber, peeled, seeded, and chopped
- 1/2 coconut, chopped
- Juice of 1 lime
- Lime wedges and grated coconut to garnish

Difficulty:

Prep Time: 15 min

Serves: 6

Process

1. Peel and chop pineapple, mango, and cucumber. Reserve 1/2 cup of diced pineapple to add after blending.
2. Tap open coconut using blunt edge of a chef's knife, separate meat from shell. Using a vegetable peeler, remove the thin inner skin. Chop coconut meat into chunks.
3. In a high-speed blender or food processor, blend coconut chunks on high until finely shredded.
4. Add mango, pineapple, and cucumber, and puree.
5. Squeeze in lime juice, and continue to process until smooth.
6. Stir in the diced pineapple. Garnish with lime wedges and shredded coconut. Serve.

Grandy Kyp's chicken soup

The smell of dill, garlic, and chicken that fills the kitchen when this soup simmers will always remind me of my Grandy Kyp. The original recipe, created by my Grandy's Bubbe, used an entire roasting chicken for some very healing bone broth! I will gladly enjoy this soup any day of the week, but it is particularly comforting when I am not feeling my best.

—Hayley

Ingredients

- 5 boneless, skinless chicken breasts
- 1 large onion
- 3 quarts chicken stock
- Garlic powder
- Pepper to taste
- Dill weed to taste
- 2 cups celery, chopped
- 1 cup baby carrots

Difficulty: / / /

Prep Time: 15 min

Cook Time: 1.5 hrs

Serves: 8

Process

1. Rinse chicken breast and place in a large soup pot.
2. Chop whole onion into bite-size pieces and place into soup pot.
3. Pour in chicken broth and season with garlic powder, pepper, and dill weed.
4. Turn burner onto medium and bring soup to a boil.
5. Reduce heat to simmer, cover and cook for 30 minutes.
6. After 30 minutes add in celery and baby carrots and cook for another 45 minutes to an hour.

Mutton stew

This hearty lamb soup is the perfect comfort food on a chilly evening. The flavors of thyme, rosemary, and garlic will fill your home with wonderful warm smells as this soup cooks on the stove. After slow cooking for hours, the tender lamb will easily fall apart with each bite of this delicious stew.

Ingredients

- 3-4 lb leg of lamb
- 2 tsp coconut oil
- 3 leeks, chopped, dark green tips discarded
- 1 fist garlic, roughly chopped
- Salt and pepper to taste
- 3-4 sprigs thyme
- 2 sprigs rosemary
- 5 large carrots, chopped
- 5 stalks celery, chopped
- 1 qt beef broth

Difficulty: ///

Prep Time: 30 min

Cook Time: 4-6 hrs

Serves: 6

Process

1. Trim silver skin and excess fat from lamb leg. Cut into 1/2-inch cubes (bite sized), and set aside.
2. Heat a skillet over medium heat with 1 teaspoon coconut oil, and sauté leeks and garlic for approximately 3 minutes. Remove from heat and add to a large soup pot.
3. Brown lamb with 1 teaspoon of coconut oil in the skillet over medium heat. Season with salt and pepper to taste, then add to soup pot.
4. Add herbs, carrots, celery, and broth to the soup pot.
5. Season everything with a bit more salt and pepper.
6. Bring the soup to a boil, then turn down to low to simmer.
7. Cover soup and simmer for 4-6 hours.

Notes

The lamb will release juices when browning on the stove top. These juices will add great flavor to the soup. The addition of homemade bone broth is a great substitution for store-bought broth.

Tomato basil soup

This creamy tomato soup will bring a taste of the garden to every bite. Even if you are not a tomato soup fan, we encourage you to try this soup anyway! The tomato flavor is mild and creamy, while the basil adds additional warm, sweet flavors that beautifully enhance this dish.

Ingredients

- 5 vine ripened tomatoes
- 1 tbsp olive oil
- Salt and pepper to taste
- 1 tbsp coconut oil
- 1 onion, chopped
- 3 cloves garlic, minced
- 3 cups chicken stock
- 1/2 loose cup basil leaves, sliced
- 6 oz tomato paste (1 small can)
- 2 tsp each of salt and pepper

Difficulty:

Prep Time: 10 min

Cook Time: 70 min

Serves: 6

Process

1. Preheat oven to roast at 350°F.
2. Clean and quarter tomatoes. Toss with olive oil, salt, and pepper.
3. Roast on a baking sheet for 30 minutes.
4. In a large soup pot, heat coconut oil over medium heat.
5. Sauté onion and garlic until onion is translucent.
6. Add in the roasted tomatoes, and continue to sauté for 1 minute.
7. Add in 3 cups chicken stock, the basil, and tomato paste and stir continuously over medium heat until the tomato paste has dissolved into the broth.
8. Season with 2 teaspoons each of salt and pepper.
9. Bring to a low boil, reduce heat to low. Cover pot and simmer for 30 minutes.
10. Pour soup into a food processor or high-speed blender, and puree until smooth.
11. Serve hot, garnished with chopped basil.

Bone broth

We call bone broth "comfort in a cup" This delicious homemade broth is wonderful to sip when feeling under the weather, and also makes a delicious homemade soup stock. Use this recipe as a base for creating all different types of soup stocks.

Ingredients

- 2-3 lbs soup bones (marrow, knuckle, or meaty bones)
- Purified water
- 1 tbsp apple cider vinegar

Difficulty:

Prep Time: 10 min

Cook Time: 24-48 hrs

Serves: 8

Process

1. Add bones to a large soup pot, or slow cooker.
2. Pour in enough purified water to cover the bones.
3. Add in 1 tablespoon of apple cider vinegar.
4. Cover and simmer for 24-48 hours.
5. Remove bones from broth.
6. Pour broth into a large bowl or pot through a fine mesh strainer.
7. Use immediately, or refrigerate up to 1 week.

Notes

To keep bone broth longer, store in the freezer in ice cube trays. Heat frozen cubes of broth on the stove top as desired. You can easily make poultry stock by using the carcass from a roasting chicken or turkey.

Sauces and Dressings

Some dishes simply wouldn't be the same without an essential sauce or dressing. When you want to kick a dish up a notch, pull a recipe from this section and get creative! Whether you are looking for a new salad dressing, or want to make some killer pulled pork barbecue, we have you covered.

Orange vinaigrette

Ingredients

- Juice of 1/2 orange
- 2 tbsp extra-virgin olive oil
- Cracked black pepper
- 1 tbsp orange zest

Difficulty:

Prep Time: 5 min

Makes: 3/4 cup

Process

1. Cut orange in half, squeeze juice of half the orange into a small mixing bowl.
2. Whisk in olive oil.
3. Stir in cracked black pepper and orange zest.
4. Toss with salad.

Serve with

- Fennel and orange salad (pg 250)

Greek salad dressing

Ingredients

- Juice of 1 lemon
- 1/4 cup extra-virgin olive oil
- 1 clove garlic, minced
- 1 tsp dried oregano
- Salt and pepper to taste

Difficulty:

Prep Time: 5 min

Makes: 1/2 cup

Process

1. Squeeze the juice of 1 lemon into a small mixing bowl.
2. Whisk in olive oil, minced garlic, and oregano.
3. Add salt and pepper to taste.
4. Toss with salad.

Serve with

- Greek salad (pg 256)

Barbecue sauce

This tangy barbecue sauce is wonderful over ribs, pulled pork, or chicken. Easy to make, and with no added sugars, this is the perfect primal sauce for a summertime barbecue!

Ingredients

- 1 tbsp coconut oil
- 3 cloves garlic minced
- 2 shallots, minced
- 1 tsp organic spicy (or Dijon) mustard
- 1 tsp smoked paprika
- 1 tsp chipotle seasoning
- 1 tsp ground cumin
- 1 tsp salt
- 1 1/4 cup chicken broth
- Juice of 1.5 limes
- 1 tsp pure maple syrup (optional)
- 6 oz can of tomato paste (no salt)

Difficulty:

Prep Time: 20 min

Cook Time: 50 min

Makes: 2 cups

Process

1. In a sauce pan, heat coconut oil on medium heat.
2. Add garlic and shallots, and sauté until soft and translucent.
3. Add mustard, smoked paprika, chipotle, cumin, and salt, and continue to sauté (about 30 seconds).
4. Add chicken broth, lime juice, maple syrup (optional), and tomato paste.
5. Whisk all ingredients until smooth.
6. Bring to a light boil, reduce to simmer, and slightly cover with a lid.
7. Simmer for 45 minutes, and let cool.

Serve with

- Pulled pork barbecue (pg 150)
- Grilled split chicken breasts (pg 210)

Notes

In place of the chicken broth, you can also use vegetable broth or plain water for this recipe.

Chimichurri

Ingredients

- 1 cup packed flat-leaf parsley
- 3-4 garlic cloves, chopped
- Juice of 2 lemons
- 1/2 cup extra-virgin olive oil
- 1 tsp each, salt and pepper
- 1/4 tsp red pepper flakes

Difficulty:

Prep Time: 5 min

Makes: 1.5 cups

Process

1. Thoroughly rinse parsley and remove leaves from stems.
2. Chop garlic cloves and set aside.
3. Slice lemons and discard seeds.
4. In a food processor, blend parsley, olive oil, lemon juice, and garlic.
5. Pour into a small bowl and add salt, pepper, and red pepper flakes.
6. Refrigerate until use.

Serve with

- Strip steak (pg 138)
- Breakfast burrito (pg 50)

Raspberry vinaigrette

Ingredients

- 3 tbsp raspberry balsamic vinegar
- 1.5 tsp Dijon mustard
- 1/2 cup extra-virgin olive oil

Difficulty:

Prep Time: 5 min

Makes: 3/4 cup

Process

1. Pour vinegar, Dijon mustard, and olive oil into a jar.
2. Shake vigorously until all ingredients are evenly combined.
3. Toss lightly with your choice of salad.

Serve with

- Strawberry salad (pg 280)

Mango chutney

Ingredients

- 1 tbsp coconut oil
- 1 tbsp garlic, minced
- 1 tbsp ginger, minced
- 1/2 large red onion, chopped
- 1 red bell pepper, chopped
- 2 ripe mangoes, chopped
- Juice of 1.5 limes
- 1 tbsp curry powder
- 1 tsp red pepper flakes

Difficulty:

Prep Time: 20 min

Makes: 3-4 cups

Process

1. In a large frying pan, heat coconut oil over medium heat.
2. Add garlic and ginger to the frying pan and sauté for 2 minutes.
3. Add red onion and red bell pepper to the frying pan and continue to sauté for another minute.
4. Add the chopped mango, lime juice, curry powder, and red pepper flakes. Continue to sauté until the red bell pepper, onion, and mango have softened. About 5 minutes.
5. Turn heat down to simmer, and cover with a lid until serving.

Serve with

- Grilled mahi mahi (pg 224)

Seafood mustard sauce

Ingredients

- 1/4 cup macadamia nut mayonnaise
- 1 tbsp Dijon mustard
- 1 tbsp freshly squeezed lemon juice

Difficulty:

Prep Time: 5 min

Makes: 1/3 cup

Process

1. Combine all ingredients in a small mixing bowl.
2. Top the crab cakes and serve.

Serve with

- Crab cakes (pg 220)
- Shrimp cocktail (pg 112)

Balsamic vinaigrette

Ingredients

- 3 tbsp balsamic vinegar
- 2 cloves garlic, minced
- 1/4 cup red onion, diced
- 1 tbsp Dijon mustard
- 1/2 tsp each of salt and pepper
- 1 cup extra-virgin olive oil

Difficulty:

Prep Time: 10 min

Makes: 1.5 cups

Process

1. Blend all ingredients except olive oil in a high-speed blender or food processor until smooth.
2. Once smooth, slowly add in the olive oil to fully emulsify.
3. Serve atop your choice of salad.

Mayonnaise

Ingredients

- 1 egg
- 1 tbsp freshly squeezed lemon juice
- 1/4 tsp ground mustard seed
- 1 cup unrefined macadamia nut oil
- Salt and pepper to taste

Difficulty:

Prep Time: 15 min

Makes: 1.25 cups

Process

1. In a blender or food processor, blend egg, lemon juice, and mustard seed.
2. Slowly add in the macadamia nut oil while processing to fully emulsify.
3. When the oil has all emulsified and you have a creamy mayonnaise, add in salt and pepper, and continue to blend.

Caesar dressing

Ingredients

- Juice of 1 lemon
- 2 cloves garlic
- 4 anchovy filets
- 1 egg yolk
- 1 tbsp Dijon mustard
- Cracked pepper to taste
- 1/2 cup extra-virgin olive oil

Difficulty:

Prep Time: 10 min

Makes: 1 cup

Process

1. Combine all ingredients except olive oil in a food processor.
2. Once all ingredients have blended evenly, slowly blend in olive oil to emulsify.

Serve with

- Caesar salad (pg 282)

Dill mayonnaise dip

Ingredients

- 1 egg
- Juice of 1/2 lemon
- 1 cup macadamia nut oil
- 2 tsp dried dill
- 1 tsp garlic powder
- 1 tsp onion powder
- 1 tsp cracked black pepper
- 1/2 tsp salt

Difficulty:

Prep Time: 10 min

Makes: 1 cup

Process

1. Place egg and lemon juice in a food processor. While running, add the cup of macadamia oil very slowly.
2. Add remaining spices to food processor, and blend until smooth.

Serve with

- Buffalo wings (pg 118)
- Butter garlic wings (pg 118)

Sunbutter

Ingredients

- 2 cups roasted, unsalted sunflower seeds
- 3 tbsp macadamia nut oil
- 1 tsp pure maple syrup

Difficulty:

Prep Time: 10 min

Makes: 2 cups

Process

1. Pour two cups of roasted, unsalted sunflower seeds into a food processor, and blend until you have a fine sunflower meal.
2. Add in oil one tablespoon at a time, blending each tablespoon into the sunflower meal until you have a peanut butter-like texture.
3. Add in the maple syrup.
4. Continue to blend until you have the consistency that you prefer.

Almond butter

Ingredients

- 2 cups whole, raw almonds
- 1/4 cup macadamia nut oil

Difficulty:

Prep Time: 10 min

Makes: 2 cups

Process

1. Place almonds in a food processor or high-speed blender.
2. Process until a smooth, fine consistency (this is almond meal, if you stop at this point).
3. Add in the macadamia nut oil and continue to process until the mixture forms a buttery, soft solid. Add more macadamia nut oil if necessary to achieve desired consistency.

Hayley's marinade

Ingredients

- 1/4 cup extra-virgin olive oil
- 2 cloves garlic, minced
- Juice of 1/2 lemon
- 1 tsp basil, dried
- 1 tsp oregano, dried
- Salt and pepper to taste

Difficulty:

Prep Time: 10 min

Makes: 1/2 cup

Process

1. Combine all ingredients in a jar that tightly seals.
2. Shake vigorously until mixed thoroughly.

Serve with

- Grilled chicken salad (pg 262)

"Peanut" satay sauce

Ingredients

- 1 cup sunbutter (pg 316)
- 1/2 cup coconut milk (pg 84)
- 1/4 cup hot water
- 1/4 cup coconut aminos
- 3 cloves garlic, minced
- 1 tbsp red pepper flakes
- Juice of 1/2 lime

Difficulty:

Prep Time: 20 min

Makes: 2 cups

Process

1. Make sunbutter according to recipe.
2. Combine sunbutter with all remaining ingredients in a high-speed blender or food processor.
3. Blend until a creamy, smooth consistency.

Serve with

- Chicken satay (pg 200)

Chive butter

Ingredients

- 1/8 cup unsalted pasture butter
- 1 tbsp chives, chopped finely

Difficulty:

Prep Time: 20 min

Makes: 1/8 cup

Process

1. Allow pasture butter to soften approximately 15 minutes before making.
2. Rinse and finely chop chives.
3. Gently stir chopped chives into the softened butter.

Serve with

- Skirt steak with chive butter (pg 128)

Garlic drizzle

Ingredients

- 1/4 cup unsalted pasture butter
- 3 cloves garlic, minced
- 1 tbsp parsley, minced

Difficulty:

Prep Time: 10 min

Makes: 1/8 cup

Process

1. Heat pasture butter in a small saucepan over medium heat.
2. Add minced garlic, and allow to cook for 2-3 minutes, until garlic gets golden and crispy.
3. Remove from heat, and allow to cool for a minute. Stir in minced parsley.

Serve with

- Grilled clams with garlic drizzle (pg 120)

Sesame ginger dressing

Ingredients

- 1/2 tbsp garlic, minced
- 1/2 tbsp ginger, minced
- 2 tbsp toasted sesame oil
- 2 tbsp coconut aminos
- 2 tsp sesame seeds
- 1/2 tsp each: salt, pepper, red pepper flakes

Difficulty:

Prep Time: 5 min

Makes: 1/3 cup

Process

1. Mince garlic and ginger.
2. Combine sesame oil, coconut aminos, garlic, ginger, sesame seeds, salt, pepper, and red pepper flakes in a small bowl.
3. Whisk all ingredients together.

Serve with

- Asian steak salad (pg 252)

Garlic and rosemary aioli

Ingredients

- 1 tbsp garlic, minced
- 1 tbsp rosemary, minced
- 1 cup mayonnaise (pg 312)

Difficulty:

Prep Time: 5 min

Makes: 1 cup

Process

1. Mince garlic and rosemary.
2. Add garlic and rosemary to 1 cup mayonnaise (pg 312).
3. Blend in a high-speed blender or food processor until smooth.

Serve with

- Pan-seared artichoke hearts (pg 102)

Cocktail sauce

Ingredients

- 6 oz tomato paste
- 4 tbsp horseradish
- Juice of 1/2 lemon
- 1/2 tsp salt

Difficulty:

Prep Time: 5 min

Makes: 3/4 cup

Process

1. Combine all ingredients together in a small mixing bowl.
2. Whisk together with a fork until an even consistency.

Serve with

- Shrimp cocktail (pg 112)
- Crab cakes (pg 220)

Buffalo sauce

Ingredients

- 10 Fresno chilies
- 1/2 cup yellow onion, chopped
- 3 cloves garlic, chopped
- 1/2 tsp coconut oil
- 3 cups water
- 1/2 tsp salt
- 1 cup apple cider vinegar

Difficulty:

Prep Time: 10 min

Cook Time: 20 min

Makes: 1.5 cups

Process

1. Remove stems from chilies, and slice.
2. Sauté onion, garlic, and peppers in 1/2 teaspoon of coconut oil for 3 minutes on high.
3. Add 2 cups of water, and cook on high stirring occasionally for 10-15 minutes.
4. After 10-15 minutes, add an additional cup of water. Turn heat to medium, and continue to cook until all the water has evaporated and the peppers are soft.
5. In a high-speed blender or food processor, blend the sautéed peppers, onion, and garlic. Add 1/2 teaspoon of salt, and slowly add in 1 cup of apple cider vinegar. Blend until smooth.

Serve with

- Buffalo wings (pg 118)

Mint pesto

Ingredients

- 2 packed cups mint leaves
- 1/3 cup walnuts
- 1/2 cup extra-virgin olive oil
- Juice of 1/2 lemon
- 1 tbsp lemon zest
- 1/2 tsp salt

Difficulty:

Prep Time: 15 min

Makes: 2 cups

Process

1. Pulse mint in a food processor or high-speed blender.
2. Add walnuts, and continue to pulse.
3. Add olive oil, lemon juice, lemon zest, and salt, and blend until smooth.
4. Garnish with a mint leaf or finely chopped walnuts.

Serve with

- Lamb meatballs with mint pesto (pg 160)

Smoky lime marinade

Ingredients

- 3 cloves garlic, chopped
- 1 shallot, chopped
- 1 lime, freshly squeezed
- 1 tbsp smoked paprika
- 1 tbsp cumin
- 1/2 tbsp salt
- 1/2 tbsp ground pepper
- 1/2 cup extra-virgin olive oil

Difficulty:

Prep Time: 10 min

Makes: 1.5 cups

Process

1. Pulse garlic, shallot, lime, and spices in food processor.
2. Slowly add in olive oil while blending.
3. Blend until mixture is smooth.

Serve with

- Smoky lime rib steaks (pg 154)

Citrus marinade

Ingredients

- Juice of 1 orange
- Juice of 3 limes
- 4 cloves garlic
- 1 tbsp brown mustard
- 1 tbsp raspberry blush vinegar

Difficulty:

Prep Time: 15 min

Makes: 2 cups

Process

1. Squeeze orange and lime juice into a small bowl.
2. Peel, then crush 4 cloves of garlic and add to the juice.
3. Add 1 tablespoon of brown mustard, 1 tablespoon of the blush vinegar, and whisk vigorously until combined.

Serve with

- Flank steak with citrus marinade (pg 166)

Red palm aioli

Ingredients

- 1 clove garlic, minced
- 1 tbsp lemon juice
- 1 egg
- 1/2 cup red palm oil
- 1 tbsp cilantro
- Salt and pepper to taste

Difficulty:

Prep Time: 10 min

Makes: 1/2 cup

Process

1. In a food processor, or high-speed blender, pulse minced garlic, lemon juice, and the egg, until combined.
2. Slowly pour in the red palm oil, 1-2 tablespoons at a time, continuing to blend after each addition of oil.
3. Continue to blend the mixture until thick.
4. Add cilantro, salt, and pepper and blend until thoroughly mixed.

Serve with

- Cumin-spiced chicken (pg 192)

Side Dishes

A truly great side dish plays many roles on the dinner plate: it can create a pop of color, an interesting texture, and most importantly, accentuate the flavor of the main course. The recipes in this section are versatile and can pair well with almost any entrée in this book. While we love the simplicity of roasted vegetables, we have also included some more complex recipes that will really wow your dinner crowd.

Mashed turnips and parsnips

Pureed roasted root vegetables are a delicious alternative to traditional mashed potatoes. The warm and slightly sweet flavor from roasting these vegetables makes this side dish perfect for a juicy, slow-roasted cut of meat.

Ingredients

- 2 cups turnips, chopped
- 3 cup parsnips, chopped
- 1 onion, chopped
- 3 tbsp extra-virgin olive oil
- Salt and pepper to taste

Difficulty:

Prep Time: 20 min

Cook Time: 45 min

Serves: 4

Process

1. Preheat oven to roast at 400°F.
2. Rinse and chop turnips, parsnips, and onion.
3. Toss with olive oil, salt, and pepper.
4. Spread out evenly on a roasting pan.
5. Roast at 400°F for 45 min.
6. Puree vegetables in high-speed blender or food processor until smooth.

Notes

Keep an eye on these to ensure that they do not burn. It is best to stir them every 15 minutes to ensure even cooking.

Sautéed cabbage

Ingredients

- 1/4 medium cabbage, thinly sliced
- 1 tbsp coconut oil
- Salt and pepper to taste

Difficulty:

Prep Time: 10 min

Cook Time: 5 min

Serves: 2

Process

1. Peel off the loose exterior layers (1–3 leaves) of the cabbage and discard.
2. Thinly slice the cabbage, working from the outside in. The core is to be avoided.
3. Rinse cabbage under cold water in a colander and shake dry.
4. Heat a large skillet over medium-high heat.
5. Add coconut oil to skillet, then add in the cabbage. Toss to evenly distribute coconut oil on cabbage.
6. Sprinkle salt and pepper to taste.
7. Cook for approximately 5 minutes, stirring frequently.

Roasted rosemary beets

Ingredients

- 3 large beets, chopped
- 2 tbsp extra-virgin olive oil
- Salt and pepper to taste
- 2 tbsp fresh rosemary, chopped

Difficulty:

Prep Time: 10 min

Cook Time: 35 min

Serves: 2

Process

1. Preheat the oven to roast at 400°F.
2. In a baking dish, toss beets in olive oil, salt, pepper, and rosemary.
3. Roast beets for 35 minutes, or until crispy on the outside and tender in the center.

Grilled asparagus

Ingredients

- 1 lb asparagus
- 1 tbsp extra-virgin olive oil
- Salt and pepper to taste

Difficulty:

Prep Time: 5 min

Cook Time: 5 min

Serves: 2-4

Process

1. Preheat grill to medium-high heat.
2. Rinse asparagus under cold water.
3. Grasp asparagus spears near the tip and base. Bend tips together until spears naturally snap. Discard bottom portions.
4. Toss asparagus spears with olive oil. Sprinkle with salt and pepper.
5. Lay asparagus on grill across the grates, or in a grill basket.
6. Grill for 5 minutes, rolling occasionally to cook evenly.

Roasted baby carrots

Ingredients

- 1 lb organic baby carrots
- 2 tbsp extra-virgin olive oil
- Salt and pepper to taste

Difficulty:

Prep Time: 5 min

Cook Time: 30 min

Serves: 2-4

Process

1. Preheat oven to 400°F.
2. Place baby carrots in a baking dish.
3. Toss carrots in olive oil, salt, and pepper until evenly coated.
4. Roast at 400°F until carrots are soft when prodded with a fork—approximately 30 minutes.

Balsamic onions

Ingredients

- 1 whole red onion
- 1 tbsp extra-virgin olive oil
- Salt and pepper to taste
- 1 tbsp balsamic vinegar

Difficulty:

Prep Time: 10 min

Cook Time: 30 min

Serves: 2-4

Process

1. Preheat oven to roast at 400°F.
2. Remove outer layer of onion.
3. Thinly slice onion and place in baking dish.
4. Drizzle with 1 tablespoon olive oil. Sprinkle with salt and pepper to taste.
5. Toss onions in olive oil and salt and pepper until evenly distributed.
6. Roast at 400°F for about 30 minutes, or until onions start to crisp a bit.
7. Remove from oven and toss roasted onions in 1 tablespoon balsamic vinegar.

Roasted broccoli

Ingredients

- 1 lb broccoli florets
- 1 tbsp extra-virgin olive oil
- Salt and pepper to taste

Difficulty:

Prep Time: 8 min

Cook Time: 30 min

Serves: 2-4

Process

1. Preheat oven to roast at 400°F.
2. Rinse broccoli under cold water. Chop florets from stems about 3/4 inch below crowns.
3. Toss with olive oil, salt, and pepper in a large mixing bowl.
4. Place broccoli in a baking dish, and roast for 30 minutes, stirring once halfway through cooking.

Cajun sweet potato fries

Ingredients

- 1 large sweet potato
- 1 tsp each: salt, pepper, garlic powder, onion powder, paprika, and cayenne pepper
- 1 tbsp extra-virgin olive oil

Difficulty:

Prep Time: 15 min

Cook Time: 30 min

Serves: 4

Process

1. Preheat oven to bake at 400°F.
2. Rinse sweet potato under cold water. Pat dry, then cut into small spears.
3. Combine Cajun spices in a small bowl.
4. Drizzle sweet potato spears with olive oil to lightly coat.
5. Dust spears with the spice mix, then place on a large baking sheet.
6. Bake at 400°F for 30 minutes.

Cranberry sauce

Ingredients

- 1 lb raw, fresh cranberries
- 1 cup freshly squeezed orange juice
- 1 tbsp pure maple syrup

Difficulty:

Prep Time: 5 min

Cook Time: 10-15 min

Serves: 6-8

Process

1. Begin by rinsing the cranberries in a colander, and remove any cranberries that have gone bad.
2. Place cranberries and orange juice in a sauce pan and bring to a boil, stirring occasionally.
3. After boiling a few minutes, cranberries will begin to pop open. Continue to stir.
4. Once they have popped, stir in the pure maple syrup and allow to cool before serving.

Carrot soufflé

Carrot soufflé is a dish always served at Thanksgiving in my family. Always known for her delicious home-cooked meals, my Grandma Jo, graciously handed over her recipe to me, to create in a "paleo way."

—Hayley

Ingredients

- 2 lbs baby carrots
- 1 quart chicken broth
- 2 tbsp minced onion
- 2 tsp fresh lemon juice
- 1/2 cup coconut oil
- 1 tbsp coconut flour
- 1 tsp salt
- 1/4 tsp cinnamon
- 1/4 cup pure maple syrup (optional)
- 3 eggs

Difficulty:

Prep Time: 20 min

Cook Time: 45-60 min

Serves: 8

Process

1. Cook carrots until soft in free-range chicken broth.
2. Preheat oven to 350°F.
3. Remove carrots from broth and place in a food processor, or high-speed blender. Puree until smooth.
4. In large bowl, combine pureed carrots, onion, lemon juice, melted coconut oil, coconut flour, salt, cinnamon, pure maple syrup, and eggs.
5. Using a hand mixer, beat all ingredients until smooth.
6. Pour into a 2-quart soufflé dish, lightly greased with coconut oil.
7. Bake uncovered for 45-60 minutes, center should be firm to the touch before eating.
8. Sprinkle with cinnamon if desired, and serve.

Notes

Carrots may be cooked and pureed hours ahead adding lemon juice and covering tightly until ready to mix other ingredients. You also may bake the soufflé, freeze it, and then reheat it later.

Garlic and herb mashed cauliflower

Ingredients

- 1 head cauliflower, washed, and cut into florets
- Salt and pepper to taste
- 2 tbsp unsalted pasture butter
- 1 Vidalia onion, chopped
- 3 cloves of garlic, minced
- 1 tbsp fresh thyme, chopped
- 1 tbsp fresh rosemary, chopped

Difficulty:

Prep Time: 15 min

Cook Time: 10-12 min

Serves: 4-6

Process

1. Place cauliflower in a steamer basket in a large soup pot, season with salt and pepper, and steam until soft (about 10-12 minutes, test with a fork).
2. Heat 1 tablespoon of pasture butter in a nonstick frying pan over medium heat.
3. Sauté onion, garlic, and herbs until onion is translucent. Season with salt and pepper to taste. Set aside.
4. Place steamed cauliflower into a high-speed blender or food processor. Add the sautéed onion, garlic, and herbs, along with the second tablespoon of butter. Process until smooth.
5. Garnish with a sprig of rosemary, or a sprinkling of fresh ground pepper.

Grilled fruit kabobs

Ingredients

- 2 bananas
- 1/2 cantaloupe
- 1/2 pineapple
- 1-2 tsp coconut oil

Difficulty:

Prep Time: 10 min

Cook Time: 6-8 min

Serves: 4

Process

1. Heat grill to medium-high heat.
2. Peel bananas, and cut into 1-inch pieces.
3. Cut cantaloupe in half, scoop out seeds, and cut into chunks, discarding the skin.
4. Peel pineapple and cut into chunks, discarding the core.
5. Skewer fruit pieces on metal or wooden skewers, alternating the fruit.
6. Melt 1-2 tablespoons of coconut oil, and brush fruit skewers with the oil.
7. Grill skewers for 6-8 minutes, turning often to avoid burning. Remove from heat when fruit begins to get golden around the edges.

Roasted baby broccoli

Ingredients

- 1/2 lb baby broccoli (broccolini)
- 1 tbsp extra-virgin olive oil
- Salt and pepper to taste

Difficulty:

Prep Time: 8 min

Cook Time: 30 min

Serves: 2

Process

1. Preheat oven to roast at 400°F.
2. Rinse baby broccoli under cold water and place on cutting board.
3. Trim and discard the ends, and then place the broccoli in a glass baking dish.
4. Toss baby broccoli in olive oil, salt, and pepper.
5. Roast for 30 minutes or until the tops are crispy and the stems are soft.

Roasted Brussels sprouts

Ingredients

- 3-4 cups Brussels sprouts
- 1 tbsp extra-virgin olive oil
- 3 cloves garlic, minced
- Salt and pepper to taste

Difficulty:

Prep Time: 5-10 min

Cook Time: 30 min

Serves: 3-4

Process

1. Preheat oven to roast at 400°F.
2. Rinse Brussels sprouts and cut off ends.
3. Place in glass baking dish and toss with 1 tablespoon olive oil and salt and pepper to taste.
4. Roast at 400°F for 20 minutes, stirring once after 10 minutes.
5. Add minced garlic, give a final stir, and roast sprouts for 10 more minutes.

Cauliflower rice

Ingredients

- 1/2 head of cauliflower
- 1 tbsp coconut oil
- 1/2 yellow onion, chopped
- 1 clove of garlic, minced
- Salt and pepper to taste

Difficulty:

Prep Time: 10 min

Cook Time: 7-9 min

Serves: 2

Process

1. Rinse cauliflower and break away from main stem in large chunks.
2. Using a cheese grater, grate the cauliflower to a coarse texture (approximately the size of rice grains). A food processor will work just as well. Pulse the cauliflower until the desired texture is achieved.
3. Heat the coconut oil in a skillet over medium heat.
4. Sauté the onion and garlic for 3-4 minutes, or until the onion is relatively translucent.
5. Add in the cauliflower rice and continue to sauté for 4-5 minutes.
6. Season with salt and pepper, and serve.

Baked spaghetti squash

Ingredients

- 1 spaghetti squash

Difficulty:

Prep Time: 2 min

Cook Time: 40 min

Serves: 4

Process

1. Preheat oven to 400°F.
2. Using a sharp chef's knife, remove the stem from the spaghetti squash.
3. Cut the spaghetti squash in half, beginning at the top where the stem was.
4. Scoop the seeds out with a spoon.
5. Place squash halves in the oven, and bake for 40 minutes, or until the squash easily shreds with a fork.
6. Shred the squash using a fork, and serve.

Haricots verts

Ingredients

- 1 lb French green beans
- 1/8 cup almonds, sliced
- 2 tbsp unsalted pasture butter

Difficulty:

Prep Time: 2 min

Cook Time: 10 min

Serves: 4

Process

1. Rinse green beans in a colander.
2. Pour green beans into a pot filled with 3-4 cups of water.
3. Bring to a boil, and allow to boil for 5-6 minutes. Once green beans are tender, remove from heat and strain from water.
4. Melt pasture butter in a small saucepan. Add in almonds once melted, and cook over medium-low heat for 3-4 minutes.
5. Add the green beans to the sauce pan, and toss to evenly distribute butter and almonds.

Sautéed spinach

Ingredients

- 1 tbsp unsalted pasture butter
- 2 cloves garlic, minced
- 4 cups organic baby spinach
- Salt and pepper to taste

Difficulty:

Prep Time: 5 min

Cook Time: 5-7 min

Serves: 2

Process

1. Heat butter over medium heat in a nonstick frying pan.
2. Add garlic to the pan and sauté for 30 seconds.
3. Add spinach, season with salt and pepper, and sauté until spinach is wilted.

Ratatouille

The full name for this French side dish is Ratatouille Niçoise. There is a lot of debate on the execution of this dish, but for our recipe we kept it simple by baking the colorful array of vegetables, seasoned simply with herbs de Provence. To finish the dish, we then plate it over our fresh tomato sauce.

Ingredients

- 3 cloves garlic, minced
- 1 yellow onion, chopped
- 5 vine-ripe tomatoes, chopped
- 1 tbsp fresh basil, chopped
- 4 tbsp extra-virgin olive oil
- Salt to taste
- 1 small eggplant, thinly sliced
- 1 zucchini, thinly sliced
- 1 yellow squash, thinly sliced
- 1 red bell pepper, thinly sliced
- Herbs de Provence, to taste

Difficulty:
Prep Time: 15 min
Cook Time: 35 min
Serves: 4-6

Process

1. Heat oven to roast at 400°F.
2. In a heavy sauce pan, sauté garlic, onion, tomatoes and basil in 1 tbsp olive oil, until soft.
3. Bring sauce to a light boil, add a pinch or two of salt, turn down to a simmer, and cover until the roasting vegetables are finished.
4. Toss sliced vegetables in 3 tbsp of olive oil.
5. Sprinkle generously with herbs de Provence and salt to taste.
6. Arrange on a baking sheet, alternating the varying types of vegetable slices.
7. Bake vegetables for 25 minutes until vegetables become slightly golden around the edges.
8. Serve vegetable slices over the tomato sauce, and garnish with a sprig of fresh basil.

Grilled vegetables

Ingredients

- 1 cup each of chopped: broccoli, red pepper, yellow pepper, onion, zucchini, and mushrooms
- 2 tbsp extra-virgin olive oil
- Salt and pepper to taste

Difficulty:

Prep Time: 15 min

Cook Time: 15-20 min

Serves: 4

Process

1. Heat grill to high heat.
2. Rinse and chop all vegetables.
3. Place vegetables in a large mixing bowl. Drizzle with olive oil and toss to coat. Repeat as necessary until all vegetables are lightly coated with olive oil.
4. Sprinkle vegetables with salt and cracked black pepper. Toss and repeat as necessary until evenly distributed.
5. Grill vegetables in a grill basket for 15-20 minutes over high heat. Stir mixture once every 4 minutes to evenly cook vegetables.

Grilled fennel

Ingredients

- 2 fennel bulbs
- 1 tbsp extra-virgin olive oil
- Salt and pepper to taste

Difficulty:

Prep Time: 5-10 min

Cook Time: 20 min

Serves: 4

Process

1. Heat grill to medium-high heat.
2. Chop any fronds from the top of the fennel bulbs.
3. Trim the base of the fennel, and cut in half lengthwise and remove the core.
4. Chop into small pieces of equal sizes. If you have a mandoline, slice the fennel 1/4 inch thick.
5. Toss fennel with olive oil, salt, and pepper.
6. Place fennel slices in a grill basket, and grill for 20 minutes. Turn fennel periodically to cook evenly.

Treats and Cheats

Well, you've finally made it to the chapter in this book that will undoubtedly make you salivate just a bit more than the others.

Not so fast!

Did you think you'd find some magical desserts back here, carrying the "paleo" label, that you could eat without an ounce of guilt? We hate to burst your bubble, but a dessert is still a dessert. These [utterly delicious] recipes are included in this book because they follow the principles of a grain-free diet, though they are not considered "paleo" (hence being labeled as treats and cheats). We believe that birthdays, holidays, and special occasions should be duly celebrated with delicious treats. In our minds, the best option for that is to have grain-free desserts that are sweetened naturally. Enjoy these recipes as you would any other dessert: in moderation.

Chocolate chip cookies

We wanted to kick off our treats and cheats section with the quintessential treat, chocolate chip cookies. These cookies are irresistible—soft, chewy, and best served fresh out of the oven. Try them with a fresh glass of coconut milk!

Ingredients

- 3 cups blanched almond flour
- 1 tsp baking soda
- 1 tsp salt
- 2 eggs
- 1/2 cup pure maple syrup
- 1 tsp vanilla extract
- 1/2 cup coconut oil, unrefined
- 1.5 cups 72% dark chocolate chips

Difficulty:

Prep Time: 10 min

Cook Time: 15 min

Makes: 24 cookies

Process

1. Preheat oven to 375°F.
2. In a medium-sized mixing bowl combine dry ingredients.
3. In a small mixing bowl beat eggs, maple syrup, and vanilla extract with a hand mixer.
4. Pour wet ingredients into dry and beat with hand mixer until combined.
5. Melt coconut oil, pour into batter, and continue to blend until combined.
6. Stir in chocolate chips.
7. On a parchment-lined baking sheet, drop balls of cookie dough, about a tablespoon in size.
8. Bake for 15 minutes.
9. Let cool and serve.

Serve with

- Coconut milk (pg 84)

Gingerbread cookies

Gingerbread cookies are a favorite holiday treat of mine that I've enjoyed my whole life. The crisp, yet chewy texture of our cookies is a perfect analogue to conventional recipes. We've shared these with non-paleo family members, and they have been given unanimous approval.

—Bill

Ingredients

- 1/2 cup molasses (see notes)
- 1/4 cup pure maple syrup
- 3 tbsp palm shortening
- 1 tbsp coconut milk
- 3 cups blanched almond flour
- 1/2 tsp cinnamon
- 1/2 tsp ground ginger
- 1/2 tsp ground cloves
- 1/2 tsp ground nutmeg
- 1/2 tsp salt
- 1/2 tsp baking soda

Difficulty:

Prep Time: 45 min

Cook Time: 10 min

Makes: 12 cookies

Process

1. Preheat oven to 350°F.
2. In a sauce pan, heat molasses to a boil.
3. Add maple syrup, palm shortening, and coconut milk to sauce pan.
4. Stir ingredients until combined, then remove from heat.
5. In a small bowl, combine all dry ingredients.
6. Pour dry ingredients into wet, and stir until batter is fully blended.
7. Refrigerate dough for 20 minutes.
8. Roll out dough between two sheets of parchment paper, until about 1/4 inch thick.
9. Cut batter with cookie cutters of choice.
10. Bake for 10 minutes on a parchment-lined cookie sheet.
11. Let cool, decorate as desired, and enjoy.

Notes

If you have an aversion to molasses, another option would be to use maple syrup or yacon syrup, although the molasses is a key ingredient to getting the classic "gingerbread cookie" flavor and color.

N'oatmeal raisin cookies

With a hearty texture and just a hint of sweetness, these cookies are the perfect treat for someone with a primal palate. These delicious little cookies are just like traditional oatmeal cookies, but without any junky ingredients.

Ingredients

- 2 cups almond meal
- 1/2 cup flax seed meal
- 1/2 cup unsweetened, shredded coconut
- 1/2 cup raw sunflower seeds
- 1/2 cup raw pumpkin seeds
- 1 tbsp cinnamon
- 1 tsp salt
- 1 tsp baking soda
- 2 eggs
- 1/2 cup pure maple syrup
- 1 tsp vanilla extract
- 1/2 cup coconut oil
- 1 cup raisins

Difficulty:

Prep Time: 10 min

Cook Time: 15 min

Makes: 12 cookies

Process

1. Preheat oven to 325°F.
2. In a large mixing bowl, combine dry ingredients.
3. In a small mixing bowl, combine eggs, maple syrup, vanilla extract, and melted coconut oil with a hand mixer.
4. Stir wet ingredients into dry ingredients.
5. Stir in 1 cup raisins.
6. On a parchment lined baking sheet, drop tablespoon-sized amounts of cookie batter.
7. Bake the cookies for 15 minutes.
8. Allow cookies to cool and serve.

"Infamous" bacon cookies

If you have never thought to add crisp, smoky bacon to a sweet treat, think again! This recipe came to us upon request, and although we thought it odd at first, they quickly came to be our favorite grain-free treat yet. When bacon is in the mix, you really can't go wrong!

Ingredients

- 5 slices nitrate-free bacon
- 1/4 cup pure maple syrup
- 3 cups blanched almond flour
- 1 tsp baking soda
- 1 tsp salt
- 2 eggs
- 1/2 cup pure maple syrup
- 1 tsp vanilla extract
- 1/2 cup coconut oil, unrefined
- 1.5 cups 72% dark chocolate chips

Difficulty:

Prep Time: 20

Cook Time: 35

Makes: 24 cookies

Process

1. Preheat oven to bake at 350°F.
2. In a medium size mixing bowl, toss bacon in 1/4 cup maple syrup.
3. Lay bacon on a parchment-lined baking sheet.
4. Bake for 20 minutes.
5. Remove bacon from oven, and allow to cool.
6. Crumble candied bacon for cookie batter.
7. Heat oven to 375°F.
8. In a medium-sized mixing bowl combine dry ingredients.
9. In a small mixing bowl beat eggs, 1/2 cup maple syrup, and vanilla extract with a hand mixer.
10. Pour wet ingredients into dry and beat with hand mixer until combined.
11. Add melted coconut oil into batter, and continue to blend until combined.
12. Stir in chocolate chips and candied bacon.
13. Drop balls of dough on parchment-lined baking sheet, about a tablespoon in size.
14. Bake cookies for 15 minutes at 375°F.
15. Let cool and serve.

Fig pinwheels

A sweet mainstay in our pantry growing up were Fig Newtons. Our recipe distills the fig filling down to its purest elements, and wraps it up in a classic cookie dough. The result is equal parts gourmet and home-made goodness.

—Bill

Ingredients

- 3 cups blanched almond flour
- 1 tsp baking soda
- 1 tsp salt
- 2 eggs
- 1/2 cup pure maple syrup
- 1 tsp vanilla extract
- 1/2 cup coconut oil, unrefined

Filling

- 1 cup black mission figs, chopped
- 1/2 cup pure pomegranate juice
- 1 tbsp pure maple syrup

Difficulty:

Prep Time: 1.5 hrs

Cook Time: 15 min

Makes: 20 cookies

Process

1. To make the fig filling, soak the figs for 1 hour in the pomegranate juice.
2. Pour figs, and juice into a small sauce pan. Heat on medium-low heat until the figs become soft, stirring frequently.
3. Transfer figs to a food processor and blend, adding 1 tablespoon of maple syrup while blending. Set filling aside.
4. In a medium-sized mixing bowl combine dry ingredients.
5. In a separate mixing bowl beat eggs, maple syrup, and vanilla extract with a hand mixer.
6. Pour wet ingredients into dry and beat with hand mixer until combined.
7. Melt coconut oil, pour into batter, and continue to blend until combined.
8. Chill cookie dough for 20-30 minutes in a freezer.
9. Preheat oven to 375°F.
10. Roll out cookie dough between two sheets of parchment paper to 1/4-inch thickness.
11. Spread filling mixture over cookie dough in a thin layer.
12. Roll cookie dough from end to end, forming a long roll.
13. Slice cookie dough into 1/2-inch-thick pieces.
14. Place cookies on a parchment-lined cookie sheet, and bake for 15 minutes or until golden brown.

Notes

Place rolled cookie batter with filling in the freezer for 10 minutes prior to slicing, for best results when cutting into individual cookies.

Coconut macaroons

Coconut macaroons bring a taste of the tropics to your dessert plate. With the addition of fresh vanilla bean to this recipe, you will enjoy a hint of vanilla in every bite of coconut.

Ingredients

- 1 vanilla bean pod
- 6 egg whites
- 1/2 cup pure maple syrup
- 3 cups coconut, shredded

Difficulty:

Prep Time: 20 min

Cook Time: 15-20 min

Makes: 12 cookies

Process

1. Preheat oven to 325°F.
2. Slice open vanilla bean pod from end to end. Pressing the bean pod flat against a cutting board, splayed open, run a knife from end to end, scraping out the vanilla beans.
3. Place egg whites in a kitchen mixer and beat until stiff peaks form.
4. Fold in the maple syrup, shredded coconut, and vanilla beans.
5. Form into 1-inch balls, and place on a parchment-lined baking sheet.
6. Bake for 15-20 minutes, or until the edges get crispy and golden.

Dark chocolate cake

Birthdays come just once a year (for better or worse). This grain-free cake is a decadent way to celebrate growing a year older without fully going off the wagon. The chocolate ganache, which is kind of like a hard chocolate shell around the cake, brings an interesting texture to the cake.

Ingredients

- 3/4 cup coconut flour, sifted
- 1/4 cup unsweetened cocoa powder
- 1 tsp salt
- 1 tsp baking soda
- 10 eggs
- 1 tbsp pure vanilla extract
- 1 cup pure maple syrup
- 1 cup melted coconut oil

Difficulty:
Prep Time: 15 min
Cook Time: 35 min
Makes: 1 cake

Process

1. Preheat oven to 325°F.
2. In a small bowl, combine sifted coconut flour, cocoa powder, salt, and baking soda.
3. In a large bowl, or KitchenAid mixer, blend eggs, vanilla, maple syrup, and melted coconut oil.
4. Add dry ingredients to wet and blend.
5. Grease two 9-inch cake pans with coconut oil.
6. Pour batter into pans.
7. Bake for 35 minutes. Test center with a tooth pick—if the tooth pick comes out clean, then the cakes are done.
8. Remove cakes from oven and cool.
9. Frost the middle layer of the cake with hazelnut frosting (pg 428).
10. Frost the outside of the cake with chocolate ganache (pg 426, shown) or chocolate frosting (pg 426).

Notes

Our version of ganache tends to dry very fast. We recommend working with this quickly so that you have even coverage over the entire cake. Reheating the ganache during use is expected, and perfectly fine.

Carrot cake

As far back as I can remember, my mother has asked for a carrot cake for her birthday. This past year, we surprised her with a grain-free version, which was a huge hit. After sharing this recipe on our website, we received feedback from many followers that this was not only a great grain-free substitute, but the best carrot cake they've ever had!

—Bill

Ingredients

- 5 large carrots, peeled and shredded
- 1 cup pure maple syrup
- 3/4 cup coconut flour, sifted
- 1 tbsp cinnamon
- 1 tsp salt
- 1 tsp baking soda
- Date mixture recipe (pg 424, add 4 additional dates for a total of 10 medjool dates)
- 10 eggs
- 1 tbsp pure vanilla extract
- 1 cup melted virgin coconut oil
- Cream cheese frosting (pg 430)
- Chopped raw walnuts for garnish

Difficulty: / / /

Prep Time: 25 min

Cook Time: 35 min

Makes: 1 cake

Process

1. In a food processor, using the grating blade, shred carrots.
2. Place carrots in a large ziplock bag. Pour maple syrup over carrots and let marinate in the fridge for an hour.
3. Preheat oven to 325°F.
4. In a small mixing bowl, add sifted coconut flour, cinnamon, salt, and baking soda.
5. Make date mixture (pg 424) with 10 medjool dates.
6. In a large mixing bowl or kitchen mixer, blend eggs, vanilla, melted coconut oil, and date mixture.
7. Add dry ingredients to wet and blend.
8. Remove carrots from the fridge, and drain the excess maple syrup from the carrots using a colander.
9. Stir grated carrots into cake batter.
10. Grease two 9-inch cake pans with coconut oil. Pour batter into pans. (For easy removal, line pans with parchment paper)
11. Bake for 35 minutes. Test center with a tooth pick—if the tooth pick comes out clean, then the cakes are done.
12. Remove cakes from oven and cool.
13. Frost cake with cream cheese frosting, garnish with walnuts, and serve.

Coconut cake

Everyone received a different type of birthday cake this year. For my father's birthday, we thought we would surprise him with his favorite—coconut cake! Our coconut cake is light and fluffy with just the right amount of sweetness.

—Bill

Ingredients

- 3/4 cup coconut flour, sifted
- 1 tsp salt
- 1 tsp baking soda
- 10 eggs
- 1 tbsp pure vanilla extract
- 1 cup pure maple syrup
- 1 cup melted coconut oil
- 1 cup shredded unsweetened coconut
- Coconut cream cheese frosting (pg 430)

Difficulty: ///

Prep Time: 15 min

Cook Time: 35 min

Makes: 1 cake

Process

1. Preheat oven to 325°F.
2. In a small bowl, add sifted coconut flour, salt, and baking soda.
3. In a large bowl or kitchen mixer, combine eggs, vanilla, maple syrup, and melted coconut oil.
4. Add dry ingredients to wet and continue blend.
5. Once batter is blended and smooth, stir in shredded coconut.
6. Grease two 9-inch cake pans with coconut oil.
7. Pour batter into pans.
8. Bake for 35 minutes. Test center of cake with a toothpick. If the toothpick comes out clean, then the cakes are done.
9. Remove cakes from oven and cool.
10. Slice each cake in half to create 4 layers of cake.
11. Frost with coconut frosting in between each layer of cake.

Notes

For easy removal, line the bottom of the cake pans with parchment paper.

Raspberry torte

We celebrated our first Valentine's Day together this past year. As a part of our romantic dinner, we made this delicious torte. No, we didn't feed it to one another, but each bite was a heavenly little bit of love. (Too cheesy?)

Ingredients

- 1/2 cup coconut flour
- 6 eggs
- 1/2 cup coconut oil, melted
- 1/2 cup pure maple syrup
- 1/2 tsp vanilla extract
- 1/4 tsp salt
- 1/4 tsp baking soda
- 3/4 cup frozen raspberries
- Fresh berries and whipped heavy cream for topping

Difficulty:

Prep Time: 15 min

Cook Time: 30-35 min

Makes: 1 cake

Process

1. Preheat oven to bake at 350°F.
2. In a large mixing bowl, combine coconut flour, eggs, coconut oil, maple syrup, vanilla, salt, and baking soda.
3. Blend batter with a hand mixer until smooth.
4. Once batter is combined, fold in 2/3 cup raspberries.
5. Pour into a 9-inch springform cake pan. For easy removal, line the bottom of the pan with parchment paper.
6. Bake for 30-35 minutes.
7. Remove from oven and let cool.
8. To make raspberry coulis, puree remaining raspberries with 1 tablespoon of water in a blender until smooth.
9. Slice the cake and top with fresh berries, whipped heavy cream, and raspberry coulis.

Notes

You may use fresh or frozen raspberries for this torte. Both work fine to combine into the batter. Lightly stir the raspberries in so that they do not break up and blend into the batter; rather they should be gently folded in, and distributed evenly.

Almond fudge brownies

Our almond fudge brownies are moist yet slightly cake-like for the perfect brownie bite. These rich, dark chocolate brownies are definitely a treat for the chocolate lover. Lightly dusted with dark chocolate, you will be sure to be in chocolate heaven.

Ingredients

- 1 cup coconut oil
- 5 oz bittersweet baking chocolate
- 1 cup pure maple syrup
- 1/4 cup cocoa powder, sifted
- 4 eggs
- 1 tsp salt
- 1 tsp baking soda
- 2 tsp vanilla extract
- 12 oz almond butter, raw, crunchy and unsalted
- 1/4 cup coconut flour

Difficulty:

Prep Time: 30 min

Cook Time: 30 min

Makes: 1 (9" x 13") pan

Process

1. Combine coconut oil, baking chocolate, and maple syrup on low heat in a small saucepan until the chocolate is melted. Remove from heat.
2. Sift in cocoa powder, stir to evenly combine, then allow to cool completely and set aside.
3. Preheat oven to 350°F.
4. Blend eggs, salt, baking soda, and vanilla in a medium sized mixing bowl.
5. Once smoothly blended, add in almond butter and continue to blend.
6. Slowly add in the melted chocolate, continuing to blend.
7. Add in coconut flour and blend until mixture is evenly combined.
8. Pour batter into a lightly greased 9" x 13" glass baking dish.
9. Bake brownies at 350°F for 30 minutes.

Notes

Sprinkle brownies with shaved dark chocolate for garnish if desired.

Almond flour pie crust

Our classic pie crust is a must-have recipe for anyone who loves to bake. We use this crust for all our pie-making adventures. The flavor is versatile enough for fresh fruit pies, pudding pies, pumpkin pies, or even cheesecake.

Ingredients

- 2.5 cups almond flour
- 1/2 tsp salt
- 1/2 tsp baking soda
- 1/2 cup palm shortening
- 2 tbsp pure maple syrup
- 2 tbsp vanilla extract

Difficulty:

Prep Time: 15 min

Cook Time: 10-15 min

Makes: 9-inch round pie crust

Process

1. Preheat oven to 325°F.
2. In a medium sized bowl, combine dry ingredients.
3. In a small bowl, combine wet ingredients (make sure to melt the palm shortening before mixing it into the batter, about 40 seconds in the microwave does the trick).
4. Stir wet ingredients into dry.
5. Pat the dough into a 9-inch glass pie dish, and bake for 10-15 minutes, or until golden.
6. Remove from oven to cool.

Notes

Shaping the pie crust takes a little finesse. It takes a few minutes to smooth out the perfect pie crust; you want to create an even, thin layer. We will often use freshly ground pecans in place of almond for our pies. The warm flavor of a pecan pie crust is the perfect complement to a pumpkin pie. For this, substitute pecan meal for almond meal in equal amounts.

Chocolate pudding pie

Chocolate pudding pie was always served at Thanksgiving by my Grandma Jo. This pie is my dad's favorite, and we created our version especially for him, for his birthday. He loved every bite!

—Hayley

Ingredients

- 1 almond flour pie crust (pg 380)
- 3 egg yolks, whites whipped
- 24 oz coconut milk (1.5 cans)
- 1/2 cup pure maple syrup
- 2 tbsp unflavored gelatin
- 1/2 cup cocoa powder

Difficulty:

Prep Time: 20 min

Cook Time: 15 min

Chill Time: 2 hrs

Makes: 1 pie

Process

1. Make an almond flour pie crust (pg 380) in a 9-inch pie pan.
2. Separate egg yolks from whites. Set whites aside in dish and refrigerate.
3. Combine all ingredients (except egg whites) in a sauce pan.
4. Bring to a light boil while stirring.
5. Set aside and let cool.
6. Cover with plastic wrap and refrigerate until set.
7. Whip egg whites until stiff.
8. Fold egg whites into the pudding.
9. Pour mixture into crust and chill until serving.

Notes

This pie can also be kept in a freezer until served.

Pumpkin chiffon pie

My dad doesn't cook often, but when he does, the result is something to behold. He has been making his famous chiffon pumpkin pie for the better part of four decades. It was bold on our part to reinvent this recipe as a grain-free alternative, but after some refinement, it finally got Dad's seal of approval. This is sure to be a staple at our holiday dinners for years to come.

—Bill

Ingredients

- 1 almond flour pie crust (pg 380)
- 1 tbsp unflavored gelatin
- 2/3 cup pure maple syrup
- 1/2 tsp salt
- 3/4 tsp cinnamon
- 1/2 tsp nutmeg
- 1/2 tsp ginger
- 16 oz pure pumpkin puree
- 3 eggs, separated
- 1/2 cup unsweetened almond milk
- 1/2 cup heavy cream (optional)

Difficulty:

Prep Time: 20 min

Cook Time: 15 min

Chill Time: 2 hrs

Makes: 1 pie

Process

1. Make an almond flour pie crust (pg 380) in a 9-inch pie pan.
2. In a saucepan combine gelatin, maple syrup, salt, cinnamon, nutmeg, ginger, pumpkin, egg yolks, and almond milk. Mix thoroughly.
3. Cook over medium heat, stirring constantly until it boils.
4. Remove from heat, and allow to cool.
5. Once the pan is cool enough, put the filling in the fridge to chill until set.
6. Beat egg whites until stiff.
7. Once pumpkin filling has cooled and set in the fridge, remove from fridge and fold pumpkin filling into the whipped egg whites.
8. Pour filling into pie crust.
9. Cover pie with plastic wrap and cool in the fridge until set.
10. An optional topping is to whip heavy cream and sprinkle with cinnamon.

Notes

Dad says to "beat the hell" out of the egg whites, which is part of the secret to success with this recipe. He says, "you might think you're beating them too much, but that's just the right amount."

Lemon cheesecake

When you're looking for a sweet-something to treat yourself, few dessert options have that "je ne sais quoi" like cheesecake. On a scale of one to ten on the cheat-o-meter, this is pretty much an eleven. We're not saying to avoid this recipe, just find many friends to share it with.

Ingredients

- 1 almond flour pie crust (pg 380)—double measurements
- 8 oz cream cheese
- 16 oz full-fat Greek yogurt
- 1 tsp vanilla extract
- 1/2 lemon, juice and zest
- 3/4 cup pure maple syrup
- 1/2 tsp salt
- 4 eggs

Difficulty:

Prep Time: 20 min

Cook Time: 80 min

Chill Time: 2 hrs

Makes: 1 pie

Process

1. Make almond flour crust (pg 380), doubling the amounts to create a thicker crust.
2. Preheat oven to bake at 325°F.
3. Lightly grease bottom of a 9-inch springform pan with coconut oil, and line with parchment to ensure easy removal.
4. Press the crust batter into the bottom of the pan, forming an even layer.
5. Bake crust 15-20 minutes, until golden brown.
6. Remove crust and allow to cool.
7. Preheat oven to 350°F.
8. Combine cheesecake ingredients in a large mixing bowl, blending eggs into the batter one at a time.
9. Blend cheesecake batter with a hand mixer until smooth.
10. Pour mixture over the crust.
11. Bake at 350°F for 65 minutes.
12. Chill until serving.

Serve with

- Strawberry preserves (pg 432)

Notes

You can also keep this cheesecake in the freezer until served.

Strawberry tartlets

These strawberry tartlets are like a perfect miniature serving of strawberry pie. For these pretty pink fruit tarts, we used a cookie dough crust to hold a few spoonfuls of our fresh strawberry preserves.

Ingredients

- 3 cups blanched almond flour
- 1/2 cup pure maple syrup
- 1/2 cup palm shortening, melted
- 1 tsp vanilla extract
- 1 tsp salt
- Strawberry preserves (pg 432)
- Coconut oil to grease soufflé dishes

Difficulty:

Prep Time: 25 min

Cook Time: 20 min

Makes: 12 tartlets

Process

1. Make the strawberry preserves at least one day ahead of time (pg 432).
2. Preheat oven to 325°F.
3. In a medium-sized mixing bowl, combine almond flour, maple syrup, melted palm shortening, vanilla, and salt.
4. Lightly grease mini soufflé dishes (approximately 2 inches in diameter) with coconut oil.
5. Form thin crusts in the soufflé dishes with the dough.
6. Bake crusts for 10 minutes at 325°F.
7. Remove from oven. Depress the centers with a spoon, and fill with the strawberry preserves.
8. Bake tartlets for an additional 10 minutes, and serve.

Notes

The crust lining in the mini soufflé dishes tends to rise when cooked. Lightly press the risen crust down, then fill with the strawberry preserves. You can also avoid this, by using slightly less dough to line the dishes.

Baked apples

Warm and juicy baked apples contain all the delicious flavors of apple pie, stuffed into a convenient package. This recipe is a fun way to enjoy the wonderful flavors of apple pie without all the fuss.

Ingredients

- 2 Granny Smith apples
- 1/4 cup blanched almond flour
- 1/8 cup (heaping) cinnamon
- 2 tbsp pure maple syrup
- 1 tbsp pasture butter, softened
- 1/2 cup raisins
- 2 tbsp walnuts, chopped

Difficulty:

Prep Time: 15 min

Cook Time: 40 min

Makes: 2 apples

Process

1. Preheat oven to 350°F.
2. Cut the top 1/4 off of the apples, near the stem.
3. With a sharp knife, remove the core of the apple without disturbing the bottom of the apple.
4. In a small mixing bowl, combine almond flour, cinnamon, maple syrup and butter. Stir until the butter is evenly combined into the mixture.
5. Stir in raisins and walnuts.
6. Stuff the center of each apple with the mixture.
7. Bake uncovered for 30 minutes at 350°F.
8. Cover with aluminum foil, and bake for an additional 10 minutes.

Banana bread

The inspiration for our grain-free banana bread came from my best friend's mom, Barbara. Barbara always makes the best chocolate chip banana bread, and I knew we had to come up with a recipe to enjoy it in a way that was in line with our eating. Barbara, this one is for you!

—Hayley

Ingredients

- 1/2 cup coconut flour, sifted
- 1/2 tsp salt
- 1/4 tsp baking soda
- 6 eggs
- 1/2 tbsp vanilla
- 4 medjool dates
- 1/2 tbsp pure maple syrup
- 1/4 cup coconut oil
- 1/2 cup overly-ripe bananas

Difficulty:

Prep Time: 15 min

Cook Time: 30 min

Makes: 3 mini loafs

Process

1. Preheat oven to 350°F.
2. In a large mixing bowl, combine coconut flour, salt, and baking soda.
3. In a separate mixing bowl, blend eggs, vanilla, and banana with a hand mixer.
4. Mix the dates and maple syrup according to the date mixture recipe (pg 424), and blend into the wet mixture.
5. Pour wet ingredients into dry, and continue to blend.
6. Melt coconut oil, add to batter and blend.
7. Lightly grease 3 mini loaf pans, and add batter, allowing some room for the bread to rise.
8. Bake at 350°F for 30 minutes.
9. Let cool, slice and serve.

Notes

For variations, feel free to add raisins, chopped nuts, or chocolate chips to the batter before baking.

Dates stuffed with goat cheese

The natural gooey, sweet flavor of dates is complemented beautifully by creamy, slightly tangy goat cheese. Topped with a sprinkling of ground pecans, each bite is like a slice of pecan pie with cream . . . delicious!

Ingredients

- 12 medjool dates
- 3 oz goat cheese
- 1/8 cup pecan meal (or finely chopped pecans)

Difficulty:

Prep Time: 10 min

Cook Time: 3-4 min

Makes: 12 stuffed dates

Process

1. Turn on your oven broiler and move an oven rack to the top position.
2. Slice dates lengthwise to remove pit and create and opening for the goat cheese.
3. Stuff dates with goat cheese.
4. Sprinkle with pecan meal.
5. Place dates on a parchment-lined baking sheet and broil for 3-4 minutes.
6. Allow to cool slightly, and serve.

Coconut fudge

The flavors of dark chocolate, infused with coconut will linger on your tongue with every bite of this fudge. These are a fudge lover's dream, meant to be savored by allowing each morsel to melt in your mouth.

Ingredients

- 1 cup coconut butter
- 1/4 cup cocoa powder
- 2 tbsp pure maple syrup
- 1 tsp vanilla extract
- 1/2 tsp salt
- 1/2 cup shredded coconut

Difficulty:

Prep Time: 10 min

Makes: 1 small pan

Process

1. Melt coconut butter by microwaving on high for 30 seconds.
2. Mix all ingredients together until smoothly blended.
3. Place in a medium-sized Tupperware container lined with wax paper.
4. Pat mixture to a flat, consistent layer.
5. Refrigerate until firm, then serve.

Peppermint patties

Dark chocolate infused with mint brings a crisp, fresh flavor to the deep, intense, richness of dark chocolate. With each bite through the chocolate shell, you will enjoy a soft center of refreshing mint flavor.

Ingredients

- 1 cup 72% dark chocolate
- 1 tsp peppermint oil
- 1/2 cup coconut oil
- 1/4 cup shredded unsweetened coconut
- 1 tsp pure maple syrup

Difficulty:

Prep Time: 40 min

Makes: 8-10 candies

Process

1. Melt chocolate on low, and add 1/4 tsp of peppermint oil.
2. In a small mixing bowl, combine coconut oil, shredded coconut, maple syrup, and remaining peppermint oil.
3. Stir all ingredients until well blended.
4. With a clean, unused paint brush, paint melted chocolate into candy molds.
5. Place the molds in the freezer for 10 minutes.
6. Fill molds with mint filling, and place in the freezer for an additional 10 minutes.
7. Cover tops with a layer of chocolate and freeze at least 10 minutes, or until you are ready to enjoy them.

Notes

Keep these in the freezer before enjoying them. Keeping them frozen will allow best results of keeping their shape.

Dark chocolate almond butter bites

We both shared a love for the classic pairing of chocolate and peanut butter before we began the paleo diet. To satisfy our flavor fix of M&M's or Reese's cups, we created these tasty little dark chocolate-covered almond butter bites. With only two ingredients, you really can't go wrong with these!

Ingredients

- 1 cup 72% dark chocolate
- 1/2 cup almond butter (pg 316)

Difficulty:

Prep Time: 30 min

Makes: 8-10 candies

Process

1. Over very low heat, melt chocolate chips in a sauce pan or double boiler.
2. With a clean, unused paint brush, paint melted chocolate into candy molds.
3. Place in the freezer for 10 minutes.
4. Fill hardened chocolate molds with almond butter.
5. Paint chocolate over the top to cover the almond butter.
6. Place in freezer for an additional 10 minutes or until completely hardened.
7. Carefully pop candy out of their molds and serve.

Notes

For best results, keep these in the freezer unless consuming. The almond butter will firm up slightly, and the dark chocolate will stay cold and crisp.

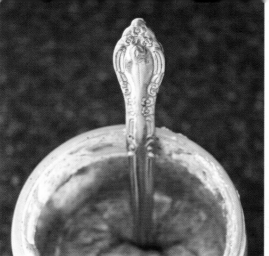

Pistachio bark

The roasted, salty flavor of pistachios surrounded by deep, smooth, dark chocolate will have your palate dancing. The flavors complement each other beautifully with the perfect mix of salty, sweet, and just the right amount of crunch.

Ingredients

- 12 oz dark chocolate (72% or higher)
- 1 cup roasted and salted pistachios

Difficulty:

Prep Time: 25 min

Makes: 20 oz

Process

1. Melt chocolate slowly in a double boiler on low heat.
2. When fully melted, remove from heat and stir in pistachios.
3. Pour onto parchment-lined baking sheet and freeze until solid.
4. Break into chunks and serve.

Notes

Store in the freezer before serving. Pistachio bark is best when chilled and crisp.

Burnt almond cupcakes

In Pittsburgh there is a bakery known for its Burnt Almond Torte cake. This is a light and fluffy two-layer cake with a middle layer of creamy custard. The frosting is a lightly whipped vanilla frosting, all topped with toasted almonds. We recreated that amazing dessert by filling vanilla coconut flour cupcakes with coconut vanilla custard, topped with vanilla frosting and toasted almonds.

Ingredients

- 1/2 cup coconut flour
- 6 eggs
- 1/2 cup palm shortening, melted
- 1/2 cup pure maple syrup
- 1/2 tbsp vanilla extract
- 1/2 tsp salt
- 1/4 tsp baking soda
- 1 cup slivered almonds
- Vanilla custard (pg 432)
- Vanilla frosting (pg 428)

Difficulty: / / /

Prep Time: 20 min

Cook Time: 35 min

Makes: 12 cupcakes

Process

1. Preheat oven to bake at 350°F.
2. In a large mixing bowl, blend coconut flour, eggs, palm shortening, maple syrup, vanilla, salt, and baking soda with a hand mixer.
3. Place muffin papers into the tray.
4. Fill each muffin cup with 1/4 cup batter.
5. Bake at 350°F for 35 minutes.
6. Spread slivered almonds on a baking sheet, and lightly toast for the final 5 minutes the cupcakes are baking.
7. Allow cupcakes to cool, then carefully remove the center of the cakes with a cupcake plunger or knife, and discard.
8. Fill the center of the cupcakes with vanilla custard.
9. Frost cupcakes with vanilla frosting.
10. Top frosting with toasted almonds.

Notes

If you don't have a cupcake plunger, a knife and spoon will do. Be careful not to remove the bottom of the cupcakes so that the custard stays inside the cakes.

Strawberry shortcakes

Our strawberry shortcakes bring the flavors of strawberries and cream to your dessert plate in the form of these cute little cakes. Each bite contains fresh strawberry surrounded by smooth vanilla cake batter, topped with our coconut vanilla frosting and a slice of strawberry.

Ingredients

- 1/2 cup coconut flour
- 6 eggs
- 1/2 cup palm shortening, melted
- 1/2 cup pure maple syrup
- 1/2 tbsp vanilla extract
- 1/2 tsp salt
- 1/4 tsp baking soda
- 3/4 cup fresh strawberries, diced
- Vanilla frosting (pg 428)

Difficulty:

Prep Time: 10 min

Cook Time: 35 min

Makes: 12 cupcakes

Process

1. Preheat oven to bake at 350°F.
2. In a large mixing bowl, blend coconut flour, eggs, palm shortening, maple syrup, vanilla, salt, and baking soda with a hand mixer.
3. Stir in diced strawberries.
4. Place muffin papers into the tray.
5. Fill each muffin cup with 1/4 cup batter.
6. Bake at 350°F for 35 minutes.
7. Allow shortcakes to cool, and frost with vanilla frosting.
8. Garnish with a slice of fresh strawberry.

Chocolate raspberry mini muffins

Chocolate and raspberry mini muffins are tasty and adorable! We enjoyed making these mini muffins together over Valentine's Day. Mini chocolate chips and raspberries fill every bite, nestled in a bed of spongy vanilla cake batter. Your special valentine will be sure to say "be mine" after a bite of these cuties!

Ingredients

- 1/2 cup coconut flour
- 6 eggs
- 1/2 cup palm shortening
- 1/2 cup pure maple syrup
- 1/2 tbsp vanilla extract
- 1/2 tsp salt
- 1/4 tsp baking soda
- 1 cup frozen raspberries
- 1/2 cup mini semisweet chocolate chips

Difficulty:
Prep Time: 25 min
Cook Time: 30-35 min
Makes: 18 mini muffins

Process

1. Preheat oven to bake at 350°F.
2. In a large mixing bowl, blend coconut flour, eggs, palm shortening, maple syrup, vanilla, salt, and baking soda with a hand mixer.
3. Stir in raspberries and chocolate chips.
4. Place muffin papers into the mini muffin tray.
5. Fill each cup 3/4 full with batter.
6. Bake at 350°F for 30-35 minutes.

Lemon poppy seed muffins

Fresh lemon fills every bite of these vanilla muffins. The golden batter with tiny black freckles throughout, contains the warm, sweet flavor of vanilla, and is accented with a fresh burst of lemon. Enjoy these with a hot cup of tea.

Ingredients

- 1/2 cup coconut flour
- 6 eggs
- 1/2 cup palm shortening, melted
- 1/2 cup pure maple syrup
- 1/2 tbsp vanilla extract
- 1/4 tsp baking soda
- 1/2 tsp salt
- 2 tbsp fresh lemon juice
- Zest of 1 lemon
- 1 tbsp poppy seeds

Difficulty:

Prep Time: 10 min

Cook Time: 35 min

Makes: 12 muffins

Process

1. Preheat oven to bake at 350°F.
2. In a large mixing bowl, blend coconut flour, eggs, palm shortening, maple syrup, vanilla, baking soda, salt, and lemon juice with a hand mixer.
3. Stir in lemon zest and poppy seeds.
4. Place muffin papers into the tray.
5. Fill each muffin cup with 1/4 cup batter.
6. Bake at 350°F for 35 minutes.

Chocolate mocha cupcakes

Who knew avocado could make such a delicious frosting? We did! This simple frosting made from avocado is the perfect guilt-free cupcake topping. You can also enjoy this frosting on its own as a pudding. Delish!

Ingredients

- 1/2 cup coconut flour
- 6 eggs
- 1/2 cup palm shortening, melted
- 1/2 cup pure maple syrup
- 1/2 tbsp vanilla extract
- 1/4 tsp baking soda
- 1/2 tsp salt
- 1/4 cup cocoa powder

Difficulty:

Prep Time: 10 min

Cook Time: 35 min

Makes: 12 cupcakes

Process

1. Preheat oven to bake at 350°F.
2. In a large mixing bowl, blend coconut flour, eggs, palm shortening, maple syrup, vanilla, baking soda, salt, and cocoa powder with a hand mixer.
3. Place muffin papers into the tray.
4. Fill each muffin cup with 1/4 cup batter.
5. Bake at 350°F for 35 minutes.
6. Let cool and top with avocado mocha frosting (pg 424).

Notes

Avocados naturally darken in color when exposed to air. This frosting, although already dark in color from the cocoa, will darken as well. Be sure to stir before use to ensure even coloring before "icing" the cakes.

Coffee ice cream

Coffee ice cream was my favorite flavor from the time I was very small. With this recipe, we successfully recreated the deep creamy flavor of coffee in a custard-like ice cream. This recipe brought back all the memories of enjoying coffee ice cream growing up.

—Hayley

Ingredients

- 3 egg yolks
- 1 can coconut milk (16 oz)
- 1/2 cup pure maple syrup
- 2 tbsp instant coffee, decaf

Difficulty:

Prep Time: 2.5 hrs

Cook Time: 10 min

Makes: 1 pint

Process

1. Combine all ingredients in a sauce pan.
2. Bring to a low boil while whisking.
3. Remove from heat and let cool.
4. Strain mixture into a medium mixing bowl, and cover with plastic wrap.
5. Chill mixture in refrigerator for 2 hours.
6. Place mixture in an ice cream maker, and run until the desired consistency is reached.

Notes

Remove ice cream from ice cream maker immediately to avoid having it freeze to the container walls. Store in a freezer until the last portion is enjoyed.

Pumpkin ice cream

With pumpkins in season, October is perfect for enjoying fresh pumpkin ice cream. This delicious treat is like a scoop of frozen pumpkin pie, especially when topped with chopped pecans and a dusting of cinnamon.

Ingredients

- 1 can coconut milk (16 oz)
- 3 egg yolks
- 1/2 cup pureed pure pumpkin
- 1/4 cup pure maple syrup
- 1 tsp vanilla extract
- 1/2 tbsp pumpkin pie spice

Difficulty:

Prep Time: 2.5 hrs

Cook Time: 10 min

Makes: 1 pint

Process

1. Combine all ingredients in a sauce pan.
2. Bring to a low boil while whisking.
3. Remove from heat and let cool.
4. Strain mixture into a medium mixing bowl, and cover with plastic wrap.
5. Chill mixture in refrigerator for 2 hours.
6. Place mixture in an ice cream maker, and run until the desired consistency is reached.
7. Serve with sprinkled cinnamon and chopped pecans.

Notes

Remove ice cream from ice cream maker immediately to avoid having it freeze to the container walls. Store in a freezer until the last portion is enjoyed.

Chocolate almond butter ice cream

I am a complete sucker for chocolate ice cream . . . all things chocolate actually. This flavor already has the chocolate thing going for it, but is enhanced even further with the addition of delicious, creamy almond butter.

—Bill

Ingredients

- 1 can coconut milk (16 oz)
- 3/4 cup pure maple syrup
- 3 egg yolks
- 1 tsp pure vanilla extract
- 1/2 cup unsweetened cocoa powder, sifted
- 1/2 cup almond butter (pg 316)

Difficulty:

Prep Time: 2.5 hrs

Cook Time: 10 min

Makes: 1 pint

Process

1. Combine all ingredients (except almond butter) in a sauce pan.
2. Bring to a low boil while whisking.
3. Remove from heat and let cool.
4. Strain mixture into a medium-sized mixing bowl, and cover with plastic wrap.
5. Chill mixture in refrigerator for 2 hours.
6. Place mixture in an ice cream maker, and run until the desired consistency is reached.
7. When ice cream is almost finished, add almond butter (pg 316) to ice cream maker, and continue to process.
8. Serve with sliced banana and chopped almonds if desired.

Notes

Remove ice cream from ice cream maker immediately to avoid having it freeze to the container walls. Store in a freezer until the last portion is enjoyed.

Chocolate chip cookie dough ice cream

My sister's favorite ice cream flavor has always been chocolate chip cookie dough. This flavor was often to be found in our freezer growing up. We knew this recipe was a winner when my sister quipped, after tasting it, that she'd like to be paid " in cookie dough."

—Bill

Ingredients

- Chocolate chip cookie dough (pg 358), omit eggs and baking soda
- 1 can coconut milk (16 oz)
- 1/4 cup pure maple syrup
- 1 tsp vanilla
- 3 egg yolks

Difficulty: ///

Prep Time: 2.5 hrs

Cook Time: 10 min

Makes: 1 pint

Process

1. Make chocolate chip cookie dough (pg 358) and freeze until use.
2. Combine coconut milk, maple syrup, vanilla and egg yolks in a sauce pan.
3. Bring to a low boil while whisking.
4. Let cool.
5. Strain mixture into a medium mixing bowl, and cover with plastic wrap.
6. Chill mixture in refrigerator for 2 hours.
7. Place mixture in an ice cream maker, and run until the desired consistency is reached.
8. While ice cream is processing, remove cookie dough from freezer and cut into 1/2 inch chunks. Remove ice cream from ice cream maker, and stir in chunks of cookie dough.

Notes

Remove ice cream from ice cream maker immediately to avoid having it freeze to the container walls. Store in a freezer until the last portion is enjoyed.

Mint chocolate chip ice cream

There is something really wonderful about the texture of frozen, yet soft, cream with the crunch of chocolate throughout. The crisp, refreshing peppermint ice cream is complimented beautifully by the deep tones of the dark chocolate chips.

Ingredients

- 1 can coconut milk (16 oz)
- 1/4 cup pure maple syrup
- 1 tsp vanilla
- 3 egg yolks
- 1 tsp peppermint oil
- 1 cup semisweet chocolate chips

Difficulty:

Prep Time: 2.5 hrs

Cook Time: 10 min

Makes: 1 pint

Process

1. Combine all ingredients except chocolate chips in a sauce pan.
2. Bring to a low boil while whisking.
3. Remove from heat and let cool.
4. Strain mixture into a medium mixing bowl, and cover with plastic wrap.
5. Chill mixture in refrigerator for 2 hours.
6. Place mixture in an ice cream maker, pour in chocolate chips, and run until the desired consistency is reached.

Notes

Remove ice cream from ice cream maker immediately to avoid having it freeze to the container walls. Store in a freezer until the last portion is enjoyed.

Date mixture

Ingredients

- 6 medjool dates, pitted
- 4 tbsp water
- 1 tbsp pure maple syrup

Difficulty:

Prep Time: 3 min

Cook Time: 1 min

Makes: 1 cup

Process

1. Place pitted dates in a microwave-safe bowl, and pour 3 tablespoons of water over the dates.
2. Heat in microwave for 30 seconds and mash with a fork.
3. Add one more tablespoon water, microwave for another 30 seconds, and mash again.
4. Add 1 tablespoon pure maple syrup, and continue to mash and stir until mixture is an even consistency.

Avocado mocha frosting

Ingredients

- 3 avocados
- 1/4 cup cocoa powder
- 1/4 tsp salt
- 1 tsp vanilla
- 1/2 cup pure maple syrup
- 1.25 tbsp ground decaffeinated coffee

Difficulty:

Prep Time: 5 min

Makes: 2 cups

Process

1. Cut avocados in half, remove pits.
2. Remove the flesh and place into a food processor or high-speed blender.
3. Add in all other ingredients.
4. Blend until smooth.

Notes

The flesh of avocados is prone to browning due to exposure to air. The frosting exposed to air will become darker in color. Stir frosting immediately before use.

Chocolate ganache

Ingredients

- 2 cups semisweet chocolate chips
- 4 tbsp palm shortening

Difficulty:

Prep Time: 20 min

Makes: 2 cups

Process

1. In a pot or double boiler, melt chocolate chips over low heat.
2. When chips are completely melted, transfer into a small bowl and let cool for about 10 minutes.
3. Add palm shortening to melted chocolate and blend with a hand mixer until combined.
4. Quickly pour over cake and spread to frost while it is still warm; when it cools it hardens to a ganache.

Chocolate frosting

Ingredients

- 1 cup semisweet chocolate chips
- 1/2 cup macadamia nut oil

Difficulty:

Prep Time: 20 min

Cook Time: 10 min

Makes: 1.5 cups

Process

1. Melt chocolate chips in a sauce pan over low heat.
2. Stir in macadamia nut oil.
3. Cool in freezer for 15 min.
4. Blend with a hand mixer until fluffy.
5. Spread onto a cake to frost.

Hazelnut frosting

Ingredients

- 1.5 cups roasted hazelnuts
- 3 tbsp macadamia oil
- 1 cup semisweet chocolate chips

Difficulty:

Prep Time: 45 min

Makes: 2.5 cups

Process

1. Place nuts and oil into a food processor and blend until you have created a creamy consistency.
2. In a pot, or double boiler, melt chocolate chips over low heat.
3. Add hazelnut butter to melted chocolate chips, then remove from heat and refrigerate.
4. Place 1 cup of chilled dark chocolate hazelnut butter in a small bowl and whip with a hand mixer until fluffy.

Vanilla frosting

Ingredients

- 1 cup coconut milk
- 1 tsp vanilla
- 1/2 cup pure maple syrup
- 1 tsp guar gum
- 1 cup coconut oil

Difficulty:

Prep Time: 12 hrs

Cook Time: 15 min

Makes: 2 cups

Process

1. Whisk coconut milk, vanilla and maple syrup in a small saucepan over medium heat.
2. Using a hand mixer, blend in the guar gum slowly until the frosting starts to thicken.
3. Remove from heat and blend in the coconut oil using the hand mixer.
4. Chill the frosting in the refrigerator overnight before using.

Cream cheese frosting

Ingredients

- 16 oz full-fat cream cheese
- 1/2 cup pure maple syrup
- 1 tbsp vanilla extract
- 2 tbsp ginger, grated

Difficulty:

Prep Time: 10 min

Makes: 2 cups

Process

1. Bring cream cheese up to room temperature.
2. Blend cream cheese, maple syrup, vanilla, and ginger with a hand mixer or kitchen mixer.
3. Use right away, or refrigerate.

Coconut cream cheese frosting

Ingredients

- 16 oz full-fat cream cheese
- 1/2 cup pure maple syrup
- 1 tbsp vanilla extract
- 1 cup shredded, unsweetened coconut

Difficulty:

Prep Time: 5 min

Makes: 2.5 cups

Process

1. Bring cream cheese up to room temperature.
2. Blend cream cheese, maple syrup, and vanilla with a hand mixer or kitchen mixer.
3. Stir in shredded coconut.
4. Use right away, or refrigerate.

Vanilla custard

Ingredients

- 25 oz coconut milk
- 1/2 cup pure maple syrup
- 1 tsp vanilla extract
- 3 eggs, separated
- 1.5 tbsp unflavored gelatin

Difficulty:

Prep Time: 12 hrs

Cook Time: 15 min

Makes: 2.5 cups

Process

1. Combine coconut milk, maple syrup, vanilla, egg yolks, and gelatin in a small sauce pan over medium heat. Stir continuously to prevent burning.
2. Bring to a low boil, then remove from heat and allow to cool.
3. Whip egg whites until they start forming peaks.
4. Fold whipped whites into the coconut milk mixture gently, until evenly consistent.
5. Refrigerate overnight before using.

Strawberry preserves

Ingredients

- 4 cups strawberries, chopped
- Juice of 1/2 lemon
- 1/4 cup pure maple syrup
- 1 tbsp lemon zest
- 1 tbsp unflavored gelatin

Difficulty:

Prep Time: 35 min

Cook Time: 10 min

Makes: 2 cups

Process

1. To sterilize mason jars, wash first with hot soapy water. Rinse, then bake at 175°F for 25 minutes.
2. Combine all ingredients (except gelatin) in a small sauce pan over medium heat, stirring frequently.
3. Bring to a full boil.
4. Stir in gelatin and whisk for 3 minutes.
5. Pour into mason jars, seal tightly, and refrigerate for at least an hour before use.

[gratitude]

A book like *Make it Paleo* would not be possible without the help and support of many great people. We want to express our sincere and deep gratitude to the following people for their unwavering commitment to our endeavors as The Food Lovers.

First and foremost, we want to thank our extended families (Aunt Justi and the kids, Jenny, Grandy Kyp, Todd and Lisa, and Caitlin) for being our strongest advocates throughout the past year. The Food Lovers had to start somewhere, and when we first began this journey, you all celebrated our every dish as if it were gourmet fare—even when that was questionable. Thanks for allowing us to indulge our creative passion, and thanks for sharing many great meals with us. Family is forever, and we love you all.

Speaking of our extended families, we want to thank the tremendous outpouring of support we've received online at our blog (www.primal-palate. com), as well as on Facebook, Twitter, YouTube, and many other sites. We cannot even begin to thank all of you that have sent us kind notes of appreciation, e-mails, and countless messages on Facebook. Your stories of success and notes of appreciation are the wind in our sails.

Tony Ryan—Thank you for always giving us perspective. You always know how to challenge us and push us further than we think we could go. Your belief in us kept us going when we thought we couldn't. Thank you for always believing in us.

Nellie and Bill Staley—Thank you for your tremendous love and support throughout our cooking endeavors. Thank you for your eagerness to try the many dishes we created, and the honest feedback you gave us that helped us refine many of those recipes. You will always be our number one taste testers.

Julie Susser—Our strongest supporter and most enthusiastic advocate. Whenever we felt lost or insecure, you were there to pump us up and remind us that we were on the right track. Thank you for keeping our spirits up, through rain and shine. You always know best.

Buz Susser—Grandpa, without your drive and passion I (Hayley) would not be where I am today. Because of you, my whole life is devoted to health and well-being. You never gave up, and always fought for what you knew was right in the face of conventional "wisdom." Thank you for never giving up, and always being a tremendous source of knowledge and inspiration to those around you.

Nellie Staley—Thank you for invaluable support, advice, and wisdom. You always have our best interests at heart, and have brought validity to our suspicion that even non-paleo people might enjoy our dishes. We love you.

Mark Sisson—You were the sole inspiration for us starting our website. The amount of knowledge you provide to those around you is inspiring. Thank you for being such an amazing source of information. You have impacted such a large group of people, and are continuing to do so. Thank you for contributing to our lives in such a way.

'Navy Mike' Weyer—Our favorite "Traveling CrossFitter." You have carried our message to over 120 (and counting) different CrossFits all over the country this past year, and have helped spread the word about who we are and what we do. We could not have done this without you, and are so grateful to have you as a friend and promoter.

Liz Wolfe—Our friend, confidant, and fan from day one. You were there from the beginning, and we appreciate that more than you know. Thank you for your honestly, sincerity, and enduring support. You are amazing, and will continue to do great things.

The Certo Family—A tremendous thank you for the use of your beautiful terrace for our cover shoot and your kitchen for some of the other shots in the book. We are so grateful to have been able to use such a beautiful space for our photos!

KC Lapiana @ In The Kitchen—Thank you for allowing the two of us to come into your store and turn it upside down for half a day to take product photos. We love your store!

Kelli Ann @ Kelli Ann Photography—Thank you for sharing your tremendous creative talent for photography with us for the cover and "couple" shots of us. You have a gift for making people look great in photos!

Samantha Gaiser—Thank you for agreeing to get up at the crack of dawn to style my (Hayley's) hair for our cover shoot. Thanks to you, my hair looked fantastic throughout the entire day, with not one bit of frizz! You are incredibly talented and we are so lucky to have you in our lives!

Erich Krauss and the Victory Belt family—In the most literal sense, this book would not have been possible without you all. We're so grateful you allowed us to create this book exactly as we envisioned it. Thank you for your excitement, input, confidence, and patience as *Make it Paleo* came to be.

Everyone else—We've undoubtedly forgotten people in all of this. If we have forgotten you, please feel free to fill in your name here: _____. We're so sorry and we love you.

So that's it for now. We hope you've enjoyed our culinary odyssey. Keep on loving your food, and one another.

With love,

Hayley & Bill

Menus for Special Occasions

Birthday Dinner

Colorful Cauliflower Salad (pg 258)

Bacon-Wrapped Scallops (pg 108)

Cedar Plank Salmon with Lime (pg 228)

Dark Chocolate Cake (pg 370)

Easter Dinner / Passover

Asparagus Soup (pg 284)

Pear and Walnut Salad (pg 254)

Stuffed Turkey Breast (pg 182)

Carrot Cake (pg 372)

Mashed Turnips and Parsnips (pg 332)

Sunday Brunch

Coconut-Nested Eggs (pg 64)

Coconut Flour Waffles (pg 82)

Prosciutto e Melone (pg 100)

Frittata (pg 52)

Thanksgiving Dinner

Rosemary Roasted Turkey (pg 176)

Cranberry Sauce (pg 340)

Roasted Brussels Sprouts (pg 346)

Pumpkin Chiffon Pie (pg 384)

Carrot Souffle (pg 342)

Garlic and Herb Mashed Cauliflower (pg 344)

New Years Celebration

The Big Game

Winter Holiday

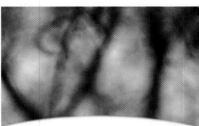

Valentine's Day

Summer Cookout

Grilled Clams with Garlic Drizzle (pg 120)

Chinese Spiced Ribs (pg 134)

Caesar Salad (pg 282)

Portobello Turkey Burgers (pg 214)

Tex-Mex Night

Steak Fajitas (pg 170)

Game Day Guacamole (pg 88)

Tacos with Jicama Shells (pg 202)

Taco Salad (pg 278)

Roasted Roma Salsa (pg 90)

Island Luau

Grilled Mahi Mahi with Mango Chutney (pg 224)

Tropical Fruit Gazpacho (pg 292)

Coconut Macaroons (pg 368)

Pineapple-Glazed Chicken Skewers (pg 216)

Far East Flavors

Chicken Satay (pg 200) w/ "Peanut"

Satay Sauce (pg 318)

Beef with Broccoli (pg 136)

Seared Ahi Tuna w/ Wasabi Mayo (pg 246)

Asian Broccoli Slaw (pg 272)

Asian Steak Salad (pg 252)

Table of Conversions

WEIGHTS

US	Metric
1/4 oz	7 g
1/2 oz	15 g
3/4 oz	20 g
1 oz	30 g
8 oz (1/2 lb)	225 g
12 oz (3/4 lb)	340 g
16 oz (1 lb)	455 g
35 oz (2.2 lbs)	1 kg

VOLUMES

US	Metric
1 tsp	5 ml
1 tbsp (1/2 fl oz)	15 ml
1/4 cup (2 fl oz)	60 ml
1/3 cup	80 ml
1/2 cup (4 fl oz)	120 ml
2/3 cup	160 ml
3/4 cup (6 fl oz)	180 ml
1 cup (8 fl oz)	240 ml
1 qt (32 fl oz)	950 ml
1 qt + 3 tbsps	1 L
1 gal (128 fl oz)	4 L

ABBREVIATIONS

Abbreviation	Long Hand
oz	ounce
lb	pound
lbs	pounds
tsp	teaspoon
tbsp	tablespoon
ml	mililiter
L	liter
g	gram
min	minute(s)
hr	hour
hrs	hours
F	fahrenheit

TEMPERATURES

Fahrenheit	Celsius
0°	-18°
32°	0°
180°	82°
212°	100°
250°	120°
350°	175°
425°	220°
500°	260

All temperatures in book are noted in Fahrenheit

Quick or Easy   Time Consuming or Tricky

[RECIPE DIFFICULTY]

Resources

Paleo and Primal Science Websites

Mark's Daily Apple [marksdailyapple.com]

Robb Wolf [robbwolf.com]

Balanced Bites [balancedbites.com]

The Healthy Skeptic [thehealthyskeptic.org]

The Paleo Diet [thepaleodiet.com]

Archevore [archevore.com]

Fuel As Rx [fuelasrx.blogspot.com]

Paleo Recipe Websites

The Food Lovers Primal Palate [primal-palate.com]

Chowstalker [chowstalker.com]

Nom Nom Paleo [nomnompaleo.com]

Everyday Paleo [everydaypaleo.com]

The Foodee Project [thefoodee.co]

Lifestyle and Fitness Websites

Cave Girl Eats [cavegirleats.com]

FitBomb [fitbomb.com]

Naturally Engineered [naturallyengineered.com]

MovNat [movnat.com]

Recommended Books

The Paleo Diet, Loren Cordain

Wheat Belly, William Davis MD

The New Evolution Diet, Art DeVany

Protein Power, Dr. Michael Eades and Dr. Mary Eades

Eat Fat Lose Fat, Dr. Mary Enig & Sally Fallon

Primal Body, Primal Mind, Nora Gedgaudas

The Primal Blueprint, Mark Sisson

Good Calories, Bad Calories, Gary Taubes

The Paleo Solution, Robb Wolf

Index

Credits

Book design, photography and food styling
by Bill Staley and Hayley Mason,
except as noted below

Cover photo by Kelli Ann Photography
Photos pgs 21, 22, and 23 by Kelli Ann Photography

Paddleboaring photo of Mark Sisson by Eric Cotsen
Head shot of Mark Sisson by Devyn Sisson

Photographs of Buz Susser by Bud Harris

Photo of Hayley and Bill on pg 43 by Leeann Marie Photography

Center photo on pg 25 by Henry Fong

Hair styling for Hayley Mason provided by Samantha Gaiser

Location for cover shot and select interior shots
provided by Tom and Susan Certo

The kitchen tools and appliances shown on pgs 40 and 41 were photographed
on location at In The Kitchen, Pittsburgh

Special thanks to US Wellness Meats for providing a large portion of the
meat photographed in this book

'Our Story' edited by Julie Susser